The Gig Mafia

The Gig Mafia

How Small Networks and High-Speed Digital Funds Transfers Have Changed the Face of Organized Crime

David M. Shapiro

BEP

BUSINESS EXPERT PRESS

Leader in applied, concise business books

The Gig Mafia: How Small Networks and High-Speed Digital Funds Transfers Have Changed the Face of Organized Crime

Cover design by Charlene Kronstedt

Interior design by Exeter Premedia Services Private Ltd., Chennai, India

First published in 2021 by
Business Expert Press, LLC
222 East 46th Street, New York, NY 10017
www.businessexpertpress.com

ISBN-13: 978-1-95334-984-2 (paperback)
ISBN-13: 978-1-95334-985-9 (e-book)

Business Expert Press Business Law and Corporate Risk Management Collection

Collection ISSN: 2333-6722 (print)
Collection ISSN: 2333-6730 (electronic)

First edition: 2021

10 9 8 7 6 5 4 3 2 1

Description

Organized crimes (e.g., weapons trafficking, drug distribution, white collar crime) persist globally due primarily to the power of modern information and communication technology (e.g., computer-based networks in the open and dark webs) to facilitate organization and the enhanced liquidity provided by electronic transfers (in effect, e-capital) to distribute criminal proceeds in the same covert and high-speed manner used by the so-called legitimate commercial enterprises. Offshore banking in tax secrecy and tax haven jurisdictions facilitates both the socially accepted process commonly known as tax avoidance, for example, and the notorious practice commonly known as tax evasion: the former is lawful; the latter is illicit.

The dirty secret of how transnational organized economic crime persists lies in global finance, especially transactions using the U.S. dollar in safe havens (e.g., the West uses the Cayman Islands; the East uses Cyprus). Regulators, monitors, auditors, and other specialists in conducting transaction review do not readily and timely tell the difference between high valued transfers that involve true sales of licit goods from high valued transfers that involve the laundering of proceeds from human trafficking, drug distribution, arms sales, and so on.

Keywords

organized crime; organized economic crime; transnational organized crime; mafia; gig economy; risk assessment; global finance; drug distribution; firearms offenses; five families

Contents

Preface

I've been providing organized crime background information and context to investigative journalists over the past several years, following stints in the public sector (e.g., U.S. Federal Bureau of Investigation, Essex County Prosecutor's Office) and private sector (i.e., management consultants, certified public accounting firms, and financial crimes specialists). After years of enjoying vicariously (i.e., observing and not participating) the multiplicity of myths and narratives with an indeterminate amount of truth in each, I decided that it would be a good time to think for myself.

Applying my experiences and refined competency in the subject matter popularly known as organized crime and scrutinizing statistical information going back at least three decades, I've come to some conclusions. Firstly, I know much less than I thought I knew. Much of organized crime folklore is better interpreted as stories of intrigue like an espionage novel wherein many individuals are slaughtered. The bible of organized crime has not and cannot be written because of a lack of not only divine inspiration but a lack of sufficient independently and impartially validated evidence. Deal-seeking defendants and career-climbing public prosecutors need not apply.

There are many useful readings referenced in this manuscript. I hope only that you enjoy it enough to follow up with the writings of so many other scholars and analysts noted herein. Finally, I wish for readers to develop an enlightened awareness of the nature of the problems inherent in the phrase "organized crime" without succumbing to fearmongering, especially where one must trust and cannot verify, and with a sense of proportion, which is commonly lacking.

CHAPTER 1

Introduction

Revisiting and Revising Organized Crime

This is a book about organized crime. It includes discussion and analysis of organizing for criminal purposes, the collective commission of criminal activities, and organized concealment of criminal activities. Relevant ideas are drawn from scholars and practitioners, including the author's professional experience. A key notion is that organizing for profit, gain, and power is not unusual; however, organizing for these ends outside of the rule of law is something extraordinary.

Please observe that within this work product, there are several related uses of the core concept of organized crime:

1. Organized crime (OC) means unlawful activities comprising crimes within the jurisdiction.
2. Organized economic crime means unlawful activities inclusive of crimes and predicate acts that could be considered criminal (e.g., whether resulting in civil or administrative charges brought by regulators such as the U.S. Securities and Exchange Commission).
3. Transnational organized crime (TOC) is a fairly recently developed phrase applied to cooperative ventures or associations, in fact among organized crime groups operating cross-border.
4. Transnational organized economic crime is a modification of TOC to include potentially unlawful activities that are generally not investigated and prosecuted as crimes (e.g., use of tax havens and secrecy jurisdictions to avoid taxes).
5. OC groups, whether restricted to collective criminal activity or expanded to collective, potentially unlawful activity.

There is a wide gulf between the land of organized crime (e.g., traditional organized crime as committed by the New York City five mafia crime families in the mid- to late-20th century) and the land of organized economic crime (e.g., bankers behaving badly, whether "mis-selling" securities and investments, wrongfully foreclosing on mortgages with defective chains of legal title, creating bogus customer accounts to meet sales targets and secure employment and bonuses). The traditional organized crime group (e.g., the Gambino crime family) is conceived as a primarily illicit collective exercise, whereas the organized economic crime group (e.g., Enron, WorldCom, Wirecard), when discussed seriously at all, is conceived as a secondarily illicit collective exercise—a hybrid. This overestimates the immorality of traditional organized crime and underestimates the amorality of organized economic crime.

Some key concepts developed in this work product include the materially misleading theory of organized crime as akin to Fortune 500 companies; the materially misleading theory of organized crime as an existential threat; the materially misleading theory of organized crime as independent of the political economy at large (including the creation of a large reserve army of the desperately un- and under-employed); and the materially misleading theory of ethnicity as a precondition to participating in any given illicit collective. In brief, organized crime is to be expected under conditions of widespread precariousness in the political economy, especially where the rule of law is changeable, whether in design or implementation, based on narrow interpretations of bribery (e.g., excluding political contributions) and honest services (e.g., excluding the prosecution of official dishonesty not resulting in bribes or kickbacks).

By way of example (and there are indeed too many to catalogue and describe), the UK's Serious Fraud Office charged two high level executives of accounting irregularities (i.e., criminal fraud) with respect to reporting profits under a contract with the UK government. While the executives were charged criminally, the corporate employer received a deferred prosecution agreement (a voluntary settlement not accompanied by a criminal conviction) (Tokar 2020a). This set of conduct is as much organized economic crime as it is white collar crime, but it would rarely be discussed and analyzed publicly as a criminal event at its core indicative of an organized criminal enterprise. In many cases and in many material respects, the conduct of legitimate enterprises are, absent the violence and extortion, functionally equivalent to traditional organized crime, except the different treatment afforded the offenders by the criminal justice system.

Traditional organized crime is interpreted as crude and characterized by the willingness to use brute force, whereas white collar crime is interpreted as comparatively sophisticated and characterized as tricksters in business attire bamboozling victims.

Moreover, any organized crime capacity sufficient to threaten the viability of a state would sooner co-opt it than consolidate it. Maintaining the legitimacy of the state is too important to risk commingling with organized crime, both from the perspective of organized crime leadership and the corrupted leadership of the state. Better to perpetuate a *kabuki* theater illusion of conflicting organizations, preserving both the alienating otherness of organized crime and the law and order regime of the state. Fundamentally, if organized crime could challenge the survivability of the state, it would indistinguishably and without differentiation become the state. Thus, if the state were to imperceptibly morph into an organized crime-like structure and operations, its residents, analysts, and scholars would likely be none the wiser.

There are two types (not mutually exclusive) of enterprises: (1) those that are supported by the threat of licit violence such as lawfully established entities that may invoke the rule of law (e.g., state or police action) to coerce counterparties, including employees, to do what they may not want to do otherwise (e.g., disbursing payments under contracts or other legal authority); (2) those that are supported by the threat of illicit violence such as organized economic crime groups that may resort to extortion or actual infliction of bodily injury to coerce counterparties, including their own associates, to do what they may not want to do otherwise. The former enterprises have the backing, explicit and implicit, of the state responsible for making and enforcing rules of law and possessing a monopoly on the use of lawful force, and the latter enterprises operate extralegally, without resort to the panoply of legal protections afforded to parties under routine contracts and other arrangements formally invoked within the given jurisdiction and political economy.

The lawful enterprise is normal, and the unlawful enterprise creates its own exceptions within or exclusions from the operation of law.

Legitimate enterprises rely on the rule of law as their explicit and immediate control mechanism (e.g., how they protect the proper disposition
of assets, enforce contractual rights and obligations); organized crime
groups rely on the use or threat of use of force as their implicit control
mechanism (e.g., extortion, murder, assault). Both forms of enterprise
reserve coercive power to accomplish their objectives. Brute force hides in
the background of legitimate enterprises, but it may be front-and-center
for organized crime groups. Legitimate enterprises use force or threats
of force lawfully under ordinary circumstances; organized crime groups
use force or threats of force unlawfully routinely. Official power legiti-
mizes the ordinary commercial enterprise under rules of law; it makes a
pariah of organized crime groups with coercive and violent power.

The usefulness of approaching organized crime under an enterprise
theory is the severity of punishment under the U.S. rules of law. Conceivably, punishment is directly correlated to risk of harm to society.

An enterprise may be three or more individuals working under a hierarchy of command-and-control for the purpose of engaging in, among
other wrongful conduct, racketeering activity. U.S. law found in Title 18
U.S.C. Section 1951 *et seq.* (as amended 2001) proscribes racketeering
and racketeer-influenced and corrupt organizations under chapters 95
and 96, respectively. Under U.S. law, there is a broad range of federal and
state crimes comprising racketeering activities, subjecting the convicted
to potential life imprisonment, with civil remedies available to private
litigants under a private right of action.

Theoretically, the punitive regime imposed on organized crime
enterprises is intended to meet the threat imposed by such dangerous
organizations. However, one may fairly question whether this threat has
been inflated beyond the evidence and data accumulated to support the
imposition of aggressive and debilitating state law enforcement action.

Interpreting organized crime as a threat to be approached as a dangerous enterprise (i.e., traditional mafia American-style derived from old mafia
Sicilian-style) is the fundamental premise of the punitive regime and forms
the basis of conclusions from the legal theories and factual concepts. If the
analyst and researcher were to take this perspective too seriously, he or she
would imagine global enterprises approaching the breadth and depth of
influence on society of the largest global corporations. This equivalency is

not observed in the world of experience and practice. Criminal networks cannot be operated like ExxonMobil. After all, legitimate enterprises file tax returns, advertise, hire and fire without resort to violence, and so on. Organized crime groups are largely opaque. The market capitalization of ExxonMobil may be transparently calculated on any given day. The pernicious effects of organized crime groups are not so clearly proven.

While it seems indisputable that command-and-control exists in the legitimate sphere of the political economy, merely taking orders under threat of violent reprisal as would be done in traditional organized crime groups is not sufficient reason to apply this fact-pattern to regional, national, international, and global cooperatives of individuals seeking profit, gain, and power outside the law (or via corruption of law-makers and law enforcement). That is, the act of taking orders does not establish command-and-control under a form of hierarchy and does not make ExxonMobil equivalent to the Gambino crime family.

However, the rule of law is an essential condition for the establishment of organized crime and its transient and semi-permanent groupings. Without prohibition of the conduct under rule of law, there is no organized crime; without official sanctioning via state-determined unlawfulness, an ill-behaving high managerial agent under the authority of a legal fiction (e.g., corporation) may be characterized by outsiders as exhibiting the attribute of organizational deviance (e.g., lack of ethics resulting in social harm but corporate and agent benefit) but not by insiders, regulators, and law enforcement agencies (i.e., his or her deviant but legal actions could be supported by peers and supervisors under the protections of the legal fiction) (Lesieur 1979, 96). (Cf. Knowingly selling overpriced investment products to vulnerable, unwitting purchasers—this conduct may be highly rewarded by the legal fiction but financially disastrous to the counterparty; it may not be deemed organized crime in the United States.)

Thus, there is a difference between a potential group of white collar criminal actors working collectively in a legitimate enterprise and organized economic crime groups operating without the cover of legitimacy provided by listing in the New York Stock Exchange. One may fairly question who harms society more—the loan shark collecting gambling debts or the financial services agent foreclosing on a mortgage without validly establishing legal chain of title, for example.

Organized criminals need to exploit vulnerabilities in the rule of law. Thus, they need to think like clever lawyers to avoid detection, prosecution, and incarceration. Generally, the rule of law is exploited through three primary mechanisms:

1. The design of the law itself contains what are commonly described as loopholes, for example, the law does not effectively cover the transactions, principals, and agents. Techniques such as the use of shell or front companies and offshore finance may render the parties immune from the reach of the particular law. Moreover, the law may allow secrecy such that beneficial owners of the asset and beneficiaries of the transaction are legally hidden and remote from law enforcement and regulatory authorities. Also, culpable states of mind (*mens rea*) may be built into the criminal law, making prosecution of certain offenses difficult to prove (e.g., those demanding specific intent to violate the law such as willfulness, which requires proofs that the suspected person knew he or she would violate the law in committing the conduct at issue). Contrast this design attribute with strict liability, under which a person may be convicted if the proofs demonstrate beyond a reasonable doubt that the person committed the criminal act; his or her state of mind is primarily irrelevant.

2. The law may not be applied aggressively in practice. Of particular mention is the protective and covert concept of prosecutorial discretion under which public prosecutors determine exclusively that which is subject to criminal sanctions (e.g., the use of leniency such as deferred and non-prosecution agreements may further limit the effectiveness of the rule of law as a deterrent against organized economic crime). Prosecutions may be aborted at other steps in the criminal process as well, for example, the presenting prosecuting attorney at a grand jury primarily controls the evidence that the jury hears—a gatekeeping function that may be perverted and unchecked by an independent and impartial authority.

3. The lack of appropriate and timely feedback mechanisms in the law specifically and society generally (e.g., the use of freedom of information statutes to obtain relevant data and evidence about the implementation of the criminal laws may be ineffective or absent).

Transparency inherently conflicts with proprietary financial interests in many cases such that the owner/controller of assets and beneficiary of profits, gains, and other revenue streams may lawfully remain beyond question and challenge. His or her remoteness from transparency may indeed lead to a condition of lawful bliss. Moreover, the public at large may be materially uninformed of the criminogenic environment, especially where some organized economic crime is highly visible in the society such as the Madoff criminal enterprise and other organized economic crime is virtually invisible (e.g., unethical and corrupt practices engaged in by financial institutions in peddling overpriced securities stuffed with too many unpayable loans evident before, during, and after the great financial crisis 2007). A public diverted is a public unable to prioritize properly.

To be truly effective in support of the public interest, the rule of law needs to be just in design, just in implementation, and just in remediation. These conditions would demand much integrity, transparency, and accountability not only from the legislative, executive, and judicial branches in relation to one another (i.e., internally), but also require significant independent capacity on the part of the governed (i.e., the public at large) to rein in and adjust errant state apparatuses. This totality of circumstances is an ideal and not a realized attribute of many, if not most, societies. A viable independent check on performance would seem a wonderful preventive and detective control on abuse and corruption of power.

Thus, gaslighting the public at large, scholars, and even criminal investigators and public prosecutors about the severity and persistence of organized (economic) crime groups based on (limited) data disclosed to the public or otherwise available through freedom of information and related transparency schemes is undoubtedly practiced to an indeterminable extent. Crime officially recognized may be dwarfed by actual levels of crime. Also, crime rates may be inflated or misleadingly presented to divert public attention from root causes of dysfunction.

The accuracy, completeness, and timeliness of the data and evidence available under the rules of law as a potential check on regulators, law enforcement agencies, and organized criminals alike is a vulnerability that may best be approached through abduction, that is, the development of educated theories and concepts not entirely dependent on inductive and deductive reasoning methods, which are vulnerable to lack of data and implicit biases, respectively. The analyst and researcher should make educated guesses to some extent based on the actual conditions of society (e.g., a plutocracy demands a different form of accountability than a democracy due to the unevenness in the distribution of power). Uncritical acceptance of preexisting paradigms, conceptual frameworks, and misleading data and evidence is not adequate.

The discussion and analysis of organized crime groups follows theory and concepts developed from official actions and reports (e.g., criminal investigations, public prosecutions) based on the state's prohibition of defined conspiratorial or entrepreneurial activities. Whether these theories and concepts hardened into rules of law are too broad or too narrow form the initial research issues motivating the preparation of this book. Scholars and analysts developing their work products under the peer-review systems generally relied upon by public officials, the academy, and private sector influencers in think tanks strive for new knowledge, but what is novel about individuals cooperating to obtain profit, gain, and power extralegally; what is novel about corruption, whether at the political, bureaucratic, or commercial levels? Sometimes, the questions are more valuable than the commonly accepted answers. Also, what if the wrong questions are asked; who benefits?

For example, organized crime is theorized and conceived as a market-based activity, that is, black and gray market participants cooperate, collude, conspire, and/or form enterprises for financial gains and political influence (cf. Lobbying). Thus, organized crime seems market-based via its participation in transactions albeit illicit somewhere in the supply and value chains. Organized crime is economic and ranges from entirely corrupt (e.g., drug cartels) to partially corrupt (e.g., legitimate business enterprises collectively behaving badly such as Enron). Traditional thought and accepted knowledge posit organized crime as market-focused (Mills, Skodbo, and Blyth 2013, 13). This may be due to an overemphasis on that which is overt and primarily measurable (e.g., punishable criminal activities like human trafficking and child pornography) versus that which is covert and primarily unobserved (e.g., implicit desires to obtain good and services more or less prohibited by rule of law under the applicable legal regime).

Linking organized economic crime to corruption, which may be conceived as collective social action that fails the tests of integrity, ethics, and often the rule of law is more useful. The market is a venue, virtual and physical, within which to transact corruptly.

Consistent with the U.S.-based (American-style) five families' conception of mafia and organized crime, the illicit enterprise is in effect an entity led top-down in a strictly enforced hierarchy of decision making and approved action. Organized crime is thus like legitimate commercial enterprises except the reporting entity is covert and supported by unlawful actions. The conception of organized crime as an attribute of society and a complement to the rule of law is underappreciated.

All societies within the modern global economy are vulnerable to organized crime risk, which results from the hazardous alignment of financial and political interests. These interests are mutually supportive to extract profit and maximize political power notwithstanding the rule of law. In fact, the rule of law squelches the competition unable to form the necessary matrix of facilitators (e.g., lawyers, accountants, bankers, politicians). The risk of organized crime to a particular society is coextensive with the ability of individuals to form relationships insulated from attack originating inside and outside of the law. Moreover, the smart lawbreaker limits his or her exposure such that, if caught, this type of lawbreaker would assert that the conduct comprising the illegality was neither willful nor criminal, notwithstanding the financial benefits accruing to the lawbreaker and harms borne by society (e.g., bankers and the 2008 financial crisis). Thus, the organized wrongdoer avoids the stigma of criminalization, becoming untouchable in the eyes of the criminal justice system (Woodiwiss 2015a, 122). This pattern is important to appreciate, as failure to do so results in gross underestimation of the influence of organized economic crime. It's not just the Gambinos.

Conduct such as price fixing, bid rigging, market manipulation, the exercise of corruption of the public sector, including the executive, legislative, and judicial branches, is not distinct in kind from actions such as extortion, offering illegal gambling, and prostitution opportunities, and drug, firearm, and human trafficking. Generally, they are corrupt. To obtain a significant measure of success and persistence, these bad actions are contingent upon an alignment of interests along the supply (e.g., manufacture of firearms and drugs), value (e.g., logistics of distribution), and return on investment (e.g., placement and integration of funds) chains and schemes. Thus, the attribute of organized crime is a composite or matrix of horizontal and vertical extension—not an organized hierarchical and command-and-control unit like the Gambino crime family.

Knowledge about organized crime cannot rest on traditional theories and conception as these do not adequately probe into the darkness of the human psyche situated in the attendant circumstances of the given political economy. Moreover, the darkness is expanded, contracted, and otherwise mediated by the political economy in place: systems that commoditize and monetize much of human activity (e.g., neoliberalism as practiced in the United States) inherently create incentives to traffic in goods and services by prioritizing market activities and transactions, that is, things, services, and influences become available for sale and purchase. Organized crime is political and economic in effect, but its causes and consequences are contingent upon the political economy in place—specifically, what is available for sale and purchase and by whom (cf. The solicitation of financial resources from loan sharks versus the preparation of a loan application to a licensed bank; moreover, what if one cannot obtain a bank loan for whatever reason, even to purchase necessities such as medical care?)

Analogously, consideration may be given to the incidence of specific infectious bodily diseases and the resulting morbidity and their relationship to the locale in which the infected is situated. Organized crime is in an important sense a public health problem solvable only through collective action. However, organized crime's adverse effects on public health are often only incidentally addressed, notwithstanding its role in undermining the rule of law (e.g., making bribery a viable pathway toward favorable official and commercial decision making) and threatening the proper regulation of goods and services (e.g., providing counterfeit items, including pharmaceuticals, that may be ineffective or worse) (Reynolds and McKee 2010, 2). The prevalence and persistence of organized economic crime as a species of corruption degrade the public at large.

Political economies that de-prioritize public goods and health may be deemed more at risk from social diseases like organized (economic) crime in a way similar to their vulnerability to infectious bodily diseases (cf. U.S. morbidity rates from COVID-19 well in excess of the remainder of the world, (Williams [Thomas Chatterton] 2020, 7)). Organized crime as a social disease may be more frequent in occurrence and more severe in influence due to the attendant circumstances in the given political economy, inclusive of the commitment to public goods and lack of commitment to providing necessary resources for public services.

Organized crime facilitates access that would otherwise be unaffordable or unattainable. This may be in the form of entrée into political influence (e.g., bribes and kickbacks) or procurement of goods or services not readily available to the purchaser (e.g., drugs, firearms, child pornography). Telescopically, organized crime creates an expanded supermarket or mall of illicit items. Microscopically, it is composed of individuals ranging from bullying thugs willing to engage in violence and threats to persons in suits masquerading as legitimate power brokers and protectors of financial and other property interests. In brief, explicit knowledge of organized economic crime (i.e., the control mechanisms in play in the upperworld) is dwarfed by implicit activities, agreements, and relationships opaquely underneath the surface (i.e., the control mechanisms at work within the underworld). There are no boardroom minutes of organized economic crime strategies and tactics.

Additionally, new knowledge and the required skills to use and further this knowledge may require the suspension of belief in the common theories used to describe crime generally and organized economic crime specifically. Constructs such as crime as individual choice, crime as exploitation of the opportunities presented in the situation at hand, and crime as routine activity learned and normalized within the criminals' milieu are useful in many respects, though these constructs are not properly theories but analytical perspectives (Levi 2010, 353). That is, they do not so much explain why criminal activity occurs as much as how it occurs. They are concepts useful to analyze the criminal activities, targets, guardians, and offenders, breaking down the criminal event into its constituent parts. Logically, they lead to either an infinite regression (i.e., if Y causes Z, what causes Y, and so on?) or adherence to a categorical and core belief in the free will of individuals. Both of these perspectives are problematic. These schemes of interpretation may erroneously compress chaotic and random activity into complex and orderly activity, that is, they may be beautiful but wrong. In fact, the development, persistence, growth, and declines of organized crime are attributable to a dynamics not fully understood and contingent upon the attendant circumstances, which are not stationary, in which individuals find themselves.

It's not the method (e.g., regression analysis) that's unsound; rather, deep, broad, comparative, valid, reliable, and timely data are lacking.

Decisions are founded on individual preferences, which are grounded in their perceived opportunities. The thinking process is both rational and irrational, transparent and opaque, and embarking and continuing on a career in organized criminal activity is a push and pull from preceding and expected factual circumstances mediated by the individual's reasoning and imaginative capacities. These vary from individual to individual. Moreover, they are not fixed categories but are formed and refined as the individual ages. Crime, especially the organized form, is not merely a matter of individual decision making but a composite of the individual's perception of items available on the menu of alternatives.

Other things being equal, organization is a beneficial capacity of individuals. Language is used to facilitate cooperation among groups of individuals more or less united in accomplishing their goals and objectives. Criminal conduct is that which is excluded from the domain of lawful protection and included within the domain of conduct formally deserving of potential sanctions: the criminal assumes the risk of lawful punishment normally imposed through the judicial system. Theoretically and conceptually, the existence and persistence of organized crime groups—locally, regionally, and internationally—should not be surprising as the rule of law imposes its own set of obstacles and impairments differentially within the given political economy. For example, not every individual can obtain an adequacy of financial resources through application to the local bank; some perceive the need for loan-sharks, whether due to bad credit histories, unexpected emergencies, and so on.

Briefly, direct and indirect participation in organized economic crime groups, whether as a complicit associate, facilitating professional, or vulnerable customer, may not comprise the dominant form of relationships among individuals in a given political economy, but it is surely not rare in the sense of being unheard of. Organized criminals are not common, but they are not consistently and awfully deviant as a subgroup within society at large. For example, criminal activities may comprise a fairly small proportion of the individual's complete set of actions (which may explain why neighbors and unwitting facilitators may have opinions of the character, if not reputation, of organized economic criminals different from the victims).

> It should not be assumed that there is anything like an organization of mobs on a wide or even national scale under the direction of "super criminals" so dear to the minds of a gullible public nourished since childhood on flamboyant film and fiction.
>
> —(Maurer 1940, 167)

While that idea was directed toward interpretation of frauds and swindles in the first part of the 20th-century United States, it applies still to interpretation of organized economic crime American-style long discussed and analyzed under the official and public prosecutors' vision of arch masterminds pre—Al Capone to post—John Gotti centrally directing and controlling vast networks of coordinated criminal activities performed as members in unincorporated criminal associations like the traditional NYC five families. An intriguing story and the stuff of even better Hollywood films, but augmented by imaginative inferences not grounded in convincing evidence. That center cannot hold, and narratives supportive of some tough-on-crime individuals' careers need critical re-examination. The bias is formidable.

In brief, a more accurate, albeit incomplete, discussion, and analysis of organized economic crime groups should focus on theories and concepts derived from analysis of large sets of loose networks and not tight, rigorously hierarchical organizations (Levi 2016, 401). Of course, the absence of a singular bogeyman or even covert small-numbered cabal that directs and controls serious criminal activity locally, regionally, nationally, and internationally creates its own problems, including an inability to explain and script organized crime groups as something more intriguing than the American mafia's five families and as something perhaps not entirely remediable by existing law enforcement tools and techniques. The source's head cannot be decapitated in such a decentralized environment. In fact, the primary earners in this loose matrix are entirely replaceable. Dispensability of leadership is an attribute supporting horizontal growth among individuals, with less dependence on wisdom from above.

However, even networks of organized crime, while not rigidly hier-archical with top-down authority effective across varied geographies globally, need to have strong local support to maintain freedom from police action and efficiency of operations (Lars and Larsson 2011, 531). Thus, in lieu of a figurative normal pyramid representing narrowly circumscribed top-down authority and power like the traditionally con-ceived Sicilian and American mafias, the more accurate representation would be funnel-like, with the narrow bottom representing local author-ity and power that expands upward throughout the network. A corrupt network conceived as a set of interlocking industries is significantly more potent and persistent than a large, rigidly operated illicit enterprise or corporation.

It is the transactional nature of organized economic criminal activ-ity that contributes to its persistence in time and diversification across jurisdictions globally. The attributes of high-tech (i.e., computer-based information and communications technologies) and digital currency (e.g., financial flows of e-money) empower individuals to pursue profit, gain, and influence outside the norm. Barriers to entry are reduced, and ivy league university degrees are not required.

Appreciation of the reality that valid records and reliable informa-tion about organized economic crime is scarce is a useful starting point for serious consideration of the magnitude and trending of this problem. Whether conclusions take the form of estimated earnings or extent of influence of any named organized crime group or family, the so-called expert and lay opinions about organized crime have definite weaknesses and limitations (Chepesiuk 2011). Sifting truth from myth and puffery is an art requiring humility, lest one too readily and gullibly accept one's own and others' conclusions, theories, and concepts independently of the skill of critical thinking applied to reliable evidence and data. Rely-ing on data and evidence that are demonstrably flawed, incomplete, and self-serving because this seems a common and familiar practice will not result in enlightenment.

Knowledge of organized crime has long been characterized by reli-ance on state-generated data and document research, especially through the use of secondary data (i.e., previously prepared by another party). Comparatively, reliance on interviews from offenders and victims, as well as the use of inferential statistics, is understandably uncommon as much about organized economic crime groups is hidden until exposed by law enforcement agencies with the narrative formed entirely or partially by their investigative and prosecutorial agendas (Windle and Silke 2019, 410–11). Thus, reporting on organized economic crime groups should result in questions about validity and reliability of the research. Moreover, controlling the narrative about the past, including the genesis, persistence, and remediation of threats to the given social order and political economy, was and is a high priority within societies, so the methodologies of research need impartial and competent analysis. This book strives for such analysis, accepting its limitations. In brief, a multidisciplinary approach may be best (Carrapico, Irrera, and Tupman 2014, 213); such is provided in this book, which focuses, among other things, attributes required to succeed and persist in the global economy outside the rule of law. It does not focus on the evil man theory of American-style/traditional organized crime.

This book takes the view that memberships in criminal societies are not the norm, but conspiracies and collusion among networks of like-minded individuals form the pattern known colloquially as organized economic crime. In brief, an organized crime group is comprised of three or more persons acting in concert to commit serious crime for financial or other benefit (United Nations Office on Drugs and Crime 2013, 2). Note that this other benefit suggests that organized crime need not be exclusively organized for financial gain but would include, for example, terrorist cells committed primarily to forcing changes in the political economy and social norms, as well as highly influential individuals seeking to move the administration of law enforcement toward other targets and priorities, whether through changes in the rule of law, appointment/election of co-opted bureaucrats and politicians, or otherwise.

Moreover, while consensus might have been reached to debunk the formerly held view of the mafia as myth (including early beliefs of J. Edgar Hoover, director of the U.S. Federal Bureau of Investigation), and there is undoubtedly a loose hierarchical structure to organized crime groups (e.g., boss, underboss), the idea that organized crime is highly centralized and coordinated is doubtful (Woodiwiss 2015b, 90). The traditional hierarchical structure imposed on organized crime, akin to the military with captains/capos, seems doubtful. While the intent of this article is not to theorize and conceive of organized economic crime as an entirely flat structure (i.e., there are often indeed levels of influence in organized economic crime groups), the idea of a rigid hierarchy like paramilitary organizations is farfetched and likely inapplicable in most modern contexts (if really ever).

Thus, the ideology behind much theorizing and conceptualizing about organized economic crime needs reconfiguration. Its operations, structure, membership, and terminology are neither loosely fixed on the paradigm of Fortune 100 companies that publicly report to the U.S. Securities and Exchange Commission nor tightly based on popular mythology often created and promoted by Hollywood, media organizations, and career-seeking law enforcement officials. Organized economic crime is not contained in permanent criminal enterprises. It flows inside and outside the rule of law in the pursuit of profit, gain, influence, and enhancement of financial and political position. It is based on terror while adopting a façade of normalcy to outsiders.

However, to be clear—organized economic crime does not need violence or threats of violence. For example, hedge fund investment advisers and/or portfolio managers using corporate insiders to misappropriate nonpublic information and thereby establish profitable trading positions ahead of the market may fairly be deemed to commit organized economic crime. A shotgun and Fat Tony are not prerequisites to commit organized economic crime.

Theories and concepts dedicated to positing an evil other or Mr. Big of certain ethnicity surrounded by others of the same ethnicity are indeed useful in bringing about the replication of crime control policies similar to those adopted by the dominant hegemony (currently, the United States), but they are not indicative of the non-monopolistic and fragmented nature of the reality of organized economic crime. In an important sense, to define the problem of organized crime in a specific way (e.g., Mr. Gambino) is to influence the acceptable solution (e.g., to counter the overblown powers of Mr. Gambino, a commensurately powerful army of criminal investigators and public prosecutors is necessary).

Organized economic crime is socially embedded in political economies across the globe, yet simplifying it as a cancerous element known as transnational organized crime permeating societies and spanning venues and jurisdictions is more mythic than truthful. What has been deemed the emotive cloud of transnational organized crime is akin to the fog of war but ungrounded in reality. There is no shadow government denoted or connoted by transnational organized crime, but there are innumerable disparate marginalized individuals from nation-to-nation that have sought and are seeking a way out of desperate conditions. These individuals organize more or less to effectuate racketeering, forming legal and illegal associations and using various means and methods to accomplish crimes (Hobbs and Antonopoulos 2013, 44–45). Expediency and not market or global dominance is the rule.

Organized criminal groups displace the state as arbiter of disputes. The macro level of statewide discipline is avoided by organized crime groups (alternatively or jointly, the purchase of immunity from effective inspection and oversight is obtained through various schemes of grand and petty corruption, including bribery and kickbacks). Instead of the norms grounded in the state's political institutions and promulgated as society wide standards by influential non governmental organizations (NGOs), the authority for organized economic crime group members is more intimate, for example, through the direct employer (meso level), with the macro level rejected. Analogously, it is as if the business code of a publicly filing corporation became the only relevant and enforceable rule of law—society be damned. One may observe this constriction of morals and ethics in the actions of individuals that contend all that matters is the employer's profit. This enfeeblement of imagination may be found in the Gambino crime family and in the market manipulating traders at Enron.

Importantly, while there are undoubtedly similarities between legitimate businesses and organized economic crime-tainted businesses, accurate and complete knowledge of how organized crime functions in practice should not be entirely reliant on the principles used in the analysis of commercial enterprises. There's much less structure and routinized processes in organized crime, traditional and new, than discoverable in legitimate reporting entities (Liddick 1999, 428–29). Moreover, the intersection and intertwining of organized crime and legitimate business, especially in the United States, make it difficult to identify consistently organized economic crime group activities from legitimate enterprise activities, that is, one's perception of the market becomes gray and uncertain (Beare 2007, 45).

Oversimplification of this dilemma of identification cannot be resolved merely by pointing to the establishment of requirements of documentation, maintenance of books and records, and deployment of effective internal controls. A glance at the enforcement actions of the U.S. Department of Justice and the U.S. Securities and Exchange Commission in relation to the Foreign Corrupt Practices Act is enough to suggest that lip service to integrity is to be expected. While organized economic crime groups lack the books and records and internal controls over financial reporting, they nonetheless need to control the disposition of assets, which, of course, implicates the use of facilitators (e.g., bankers, lawyers, accountants, company formation agents). Often, these facilitation strategies will also be used by legitimate enterprises.

Thus, the difficulties in recognizing and measuring organized criminal activities are formidable, presenting a predicament and pushing the scholar and analyst into the narratives used by criminal investigators and public prosecutors. A picture may be worth a thousand words, but a good story (e.g., *The Godfather* by Puzo) or film (e.g., *Goodfellas* by Scorsese) may be worth millions upon millions of dollars. In a sense, one does not so much follow the money as one is pulled into its vortex.

However, the most alluring and invidious characteristics of organized crime are its tendencies to corrupt and create collusive commercial relationships in the domestic (i.e., the United States) and international (e.g., South America) political economies in furtherance of power, profit, and gain. Organized crime is materially supported, if not formed, by common interests among politicians, police, business elite, and so-called rank-and-file associates, all of whom may discover that the benefits of organized crime are well worth assumption of the risks (InSight Crime 2019).

Moreover, while analysis of organized crime in comparison to the structures and processes of legitimate enterprises often comprises valuable scholarly exercises (e.g., enterprise conditions) such as supply, demand, competition, and regulation provide a high level conceptual framework for contrasting the legitimate enterprise against the organized crime enterprise (Lord, Campbell, and Van Wingerde 2019, 1229), the proverbial devil is in the details. Market dimensions such as the actors and providers, commodities and products, and services used to understand the particular fit of an enterprise within a political economy indeed contribute to understanding the big picture in a sense (*id.* at 1223), but it is the professional intermediation (e.g., company formation agents, lawyers, bankers, accountants) that provides the intersection between similar market conduct such as legitimate tax avoidance and unlawful tax evasion. Neither of these categories is exclusive to organized economic crime groups. Again, one may observe the outsized influence of criminal investigators and public prosecutors at work: tax evasion makes one an organized crime figure (cf. Al Capone), but tax avoidance makes one richer and sans criminal taint. One may fairly inquire how these distinctions are made by investigators and prosecutors, but the public disclosure and especially prosecutorial discretion often leave one required to trust too much in these officials' decision making. That is, one must trust without verification.

Perhaps not so coincidentally, by the 60s and 70s, occurring alongside the reportedly powerful influence of the American mafia-style organized crime groups, especially in New York City, the use of artificial accounting devices to exploit tax avoidance opportunities became common for the legitimate elite, including the politically exposed persons (Ogle 2020, 30). Concealing profits and gains and the covert accumulation of capital may comprise at least one important intersection of organized economic crime groups and the non criminal elite. Creating transactions and audit trails that place income and gains, whether earned lawfully or unlawfully, and assets, whether disclosed or undisclosed to tax administrations, is a playground for lawyers, bankers, and accountants that knowingly, recklessly, or unwittingly facilitate the growth and persistence of organized (crime) groups. Organized corruption, whether in the upper- or under-world, needs these facilitators to preserve the monetary value of the big score. In a sense, high tech information and communications technology facilitates these global but illicit financial flows by bridging these worlds under common goals and objectives, including profit maximization, capital accumulation, and fee income.

Moreover, conduct typically deemed tax avoidance and not tax evasion empowers the professional facilitators to deem themselves not culpable, that is, they are criminaloids whose conduct is akin to "honest fraud." They learn how to commit these honest acts of fraud within their given employer, industry, and institutions, including the criminal justice system (Ruggiero 2019, 254). Thus, it is not their raw conduct that is scrutinized with respect to the rule of law; instead, they skirt along the cusp between that which the state prosecutes and that which the state ignores, for whatever reason. Hence, their sense of clean hands arises not from the propriety and integrity of such borderline schemes as those comprising tax avoidance but from the lack of aggressive prosecutorial response from the criminal justice system. Here, we may observe the powerful yet seemingly arbitrary role played by the state in deciding which tax reduction schemes are acceptable and which are criminal.

Clearly, if an individual were to kill another without excuse or justification, he or she may be deemed to have committed homicide notwithstanding the silence and ignorance of the criminal justice system that for whatever reason overlooks the conduct. The failure of the state and criminal justice system to recognize the raw predicate acts for what they are is a form of whitewashing and processing of the raw conduct into acts that are not unlawful. This formally acceptable social processing does not change the underlying reality; criminal activities are real notwithstanding the state's failure to recognize them.

The analysis of organized economic crime needs to penetrate and expand the hegemonic market-based thinking of neoliberal economics by adding a heretofore fairly opaque and non-criminalized domain—the set of transactions comprising tax reduction strategies and offshore finance. While tax avoidance and tax evasion are not identical, they share the same reasons for existence: tax sheltering. A focus on the professional facilitators' exploitation of the vulnerabilities offered through legal technicalities, whether created intentionally as loopholes or drafted inexpertly due to careless legislators, would expose the false sense of lack of equivalence between strategies of avoidance and evasion. Arguably, preservation of assets, estates, and trusts through offshore finance and capital outflows comprise a serious threat to the national public sectors while benefiting some facilitating agents in the private sector, as well as the beneficial owners. Thus, the state's law enforcement and public policy regimes pick winners and losers without substantive justification, using legal formalism. One may fairly consider who can benefit from the legal niceties around tax avoidance and evasion strategies, and who cannot really take advantage of these protective pathways to capital accumulation. Additionally, the state that adopts such preferential policies and practices may foster a sense of illegitimacy of the ruling regime among the public at large.

This study of organized crime is not based on deductive or inductive methods of reasoning. Deductive arguments demand necessary conclusions from clearly accepted, valid and reliable first principles, which are lacking; inductive arguments do not provide robust explanations, omitting that which drives and transforms organized economic criminal activities (Douven 2017). However, this study is based on abductive reasoning to explain that which may be too often unobservable or without sufficient documentation (e.g., wide conspiracies, clandestine criminal conduct), using the principle of best explanation. Realistically, hard data are unavailable; alternative ways of knowing are required.

Sources of evidence for abductive reasoning include:

- Records obtained from criminal investigators' surveillance techniques
- Interviews of witnesses and targets
- Summary reports prepared by public prosecutors in putting together the legal theory of the case

Each of these evidence streams contributes to identifying the nodes of strategic decision making and paths of criminal activities to lead experts in the field to their conclusions about the material aspects of organized economic crime. The resultant analyses are supported by evidence, sometimes inadmissible, but they are not ordinarily provable by the methodologies common in the social sciences such as quantitative regression analysis. Fundamental considerations of whether organized economic crimes are to be interpreted as independent variables that corrupt society or as dependent variables that result from collective corruption impair the purity of analysis based on regression.

In brief, the accuracy and completeness of studies of organized crime and its structuring, operations, and governance are empirically and logically lacking in timeliness. They refer to historical conditions of detected organized criminal activities from the perspectives of biased individuals such as criminal investigators, public prosecutors, offenders, informants, and other witnesses and victims. These observed and unobserved biases cannot be measured quantitatively, but they matter greatly. Careerism bends the arc of the narrative to that which benefits the storytellers, which in the case of organized (American-style mafia) crime is sourced primarily through the criminal investigator and public prosecutor. This results in an incomplete and materially misleading interpretation of organized economic crime, leaving out how individuals in suits with the support of lawyers, accountants, and bankers can accomplish plundering of the public without resort to threats and acts of illicit violent. These actors may have the state and rule of law behind them.

To know organized economic crime is to recognize and distinguish truth from falsity (e.g., the primarily illicit, such as the Gambino crime family, to the mixed or hybrid, such as the Enron corporation, to the primarily licit enterprise, such as WalMart). Organized crime is variable and opportunistic not fixedly attached to weak states and ineffective rules of law. Concrete circumstances that risk to the surface of public attention are deceptively incomplete. They do not show the creative historical preparation occurring throughout society that makes organized economic crime the preference of both desperate and privileged individuals.

The future pathways of organized crime are necessarily abstract, avoiding description at present, transforming from revealed methods and practices that were detected by criminal investigators. However, they may be analyzed intelligently through studies calling upon the skills and methods of risk assessment (e.g., vulnerability of the target and guardian; exploitation capacity of the offender and his or her network). Organized economic crime is a collective social action that exploits vulnerability with society generally and individuals specifically.

Generally, accuracy of organized economic crime risk assessment depends on the knowledge of local conditions (e.g., leadership tends to be based on familiar and well-grounded relationships), appreciation of the comparative rarity of such underlying organized criminal activity (e.g., most individuals are not committed to workforces that focus on the provision of illicit goods or services), and market-based analysis (e.g., organized economic crime is lured by and coalesces around alpha profit opportunities) (Albanese 2008, 272).

Attendant circumstances matter in the assessment of vulnerability. A state characterized by surveillance and supporting detective and administrative systems, controls, and processes operative deep and wide (e.g., private sector snooping, intelligence agency sweeping, criminal investigator subpoenaing, public prosecutor discretion) is vulnerable differently from a state characterized by a basic lawlessness. The former has information, and the latter has chaos. However, among other vulnerabilities, the former is vulnerable to corruption of state (e.g., fascism; deleterious cooperation between public and private sectors; laws, regulations, and law enforcement not in the true public interest), and latter is vulnerable to anarchy (e.g., gray and black markets providing essential goods and services, including financial credit, lack of access to an honest and well-functioning judiciary to mediate claims and defenses).

A deep and broad understanding of the operation of variable organized economic crime groups in the particular society in the particular time is necessary to develop generally accepted knowledge and principles. Otherwise, one is lacking context, history, and awareness of the present actuality of variable organized economic crime. Epistemology of organized crime is a function of sifting through hypotheses, premises, and conclusions toward the reality of the conditions of cooperating criminals' manifest in the facts and evidence at hand (Whaley and Busby 2000, 92). There is a gulf between proximate causes (e.g., the cooperative and organized pursuit of criminally obtained financial profit, gain, and political influence) and root causes (e.g., the deficiencies in living conditions in society and governance that make cooperative and organized pursuits desirable).

There is an expression common in consideration of the design of internal control systems for economic units, including proprietary business entities and public sector and not-for-profit entities—the system should require a conspiracy to unlawfully take assets belonging to the economic unit. This is what has occurred. Currently, transactions are overseen by systems of multiple review and approvals such that rare is the case of one individual alone causing a large loss to his or her employer. This perceived organization strength can be defeated by the development of a clever conspiracy. Be careful what you wish for!

As organized economic crime is not accurately, completely, properly, and timely apprehended from the perspective of quantitative regression analysis alone (obtaining sufficient observations of reliable panel data would take too long and would be too expensive), it may be practically and expediently viewed as an outcome of initial conditions in society. Arguably, it may be posited as dependent variable with root causes within the political economy and as an independent variable with adverse effects on the political economy. These causes and effects exist at the social, institutional, and individual levels. See Table 1.1 below for a summary depiction of these attendant circumstances.

The reliability and helpfulness of these insights are not to be interpreted as absolute truths but as indicative signs within a society infected by organized economic crime, bearing in mind that trustworthy information concerning organized economic crime is rarer than commonly conceived.

In brief, the table suggests that organized economic crime creates and/or arises from a dystopia and corrupted sense of individual freedom notwithstanding the liberties entrusted to the individual by the state. The individual is not merely philosophically free in the abstract but impelled/compelled to collective action to remediate and improve his or her position and status. The socialization is likewise corrupted.

Essentially, organized economic crime is an illicit extractive process, absorbing financial resources and assets from productive processes. It has analogues in the legitimate political economy (cf. Rentier capitalism), which renders it as a useful model to study, whether as a causative agent contributing to the corruption of society or as a logical and empirical result of a political economy that leaves many behind. Organized economic crime develops and prospers under the conditions of state-sponsored

Table 1.1 Overview of causes and consequences of organized economic crime

Overview	Social	Institutional	Individual
Causes	Market failure	Ineffective law enforcement	Opportunism and social norms
Consequences	Black and gray markets	Corruption, including cronyism	Amoral, win-at-all costs perspective

capitalism (e.g., China) and the conditions of the capital-sponsored state (e.g., the United States). The use of ideology dependent on who owns and controls the means of production matters less than the process of distribution of the goods and services produced. For example, if the landlord's rents are way too high, it matters little from the perspective of the tenant whether the landlord is an individual or the state.

Thus, the question of where did organized crime begin is in material respects not determinative of where it is and how it succeeds (and fails) in meeting the needs and desires of individuals within a given political economy. Organized crime is in inherent risk in society and collective action. People getting together to conspire in the harming of another person, whether through taking his or her property by force or fraud or through manipulating executive, legislative, or judicial decision- and policy-making with bribery and other unlawful means, is hardly a recent phenomenon. The search for and realization of an unfair advantage infects political economies, especially in conditions of winner-take-all and/or inadequate social safety nets for the inevitable losers in a competitive environment.

Ironically, a highly competitive environment is prone to increasing organized economic crime risk by rivals colluding for advantage (cf. bid-rigging, market manipulation, price-fixing, customer allocation, bribery and kickback schemes—these actions against the social contract [i.e., antitrust] are more effectively performed with the cooperation and co-optation of small but well-placed individuals).

This is not to suggest that organized crime is for losers as the abilities required to become and remain successful in organized economic crime ventures demand much across the organization:

- High managerial agents (e.g., bosses and underbosses)—these individuals oversee the staff, planning and conspiring inside and outside of the gang, meting out discipline, issuing contracts and promotions, determining their financial interests (i.e., cuts of the criminal proceeds). These agents have been called bosses, underbosses, and capos, though this paramilitary nomenclature is misleading as it suggests a discipline and orderly process non existent.

- Staff (e.g., full-time/part-time associates)—these individuals earn the money, directly participating in illicit transactions (e.g., gambling, drugs, murders under contracts). These staff members have been called soldiers and associates. Again, paramilitary in too many descriptions but essential toward effectuating (rather than tasking and/or financing) the underlying criminal conduct such as making the bribe, receiving the kickback, and so on.

- Consultants (e.g., facilitators such as lawyers, accountants, and bankers)—these individuals prevent and fix problems (e.g., designing and carrying out money laundering schemes, shell company formations, arrangements for bail money and a lawyer if arrest). Consultants include the so-called consiglieres (World Heritage Encyclopedia 2020). This apparently legitimate domain (as it also serves mere tax avoiders!) is both the underbelly and upperworld of organized economic crime. It seems legit and provides high incomes for many of the participants.

Of course, facilitators may come in the most surprising forms. For example, a formerly well-respected professor from the University of Miami (Florida, United States) provided substantial assistance to money laundering activities in support of organized crime (Asmann, Dudley, and Molinares 2020). Talent, expertise, success, reputation, and skill do not necessarily raise the integrity and accountability of the human species, especially where there are fertile opportunities for illicit commissions for (illicit) services rendered. It may be that in some jurisdictions anything is for sale at the right price; this corruption supports the proliferation and persistence of organized economic crime. Really, the only criterion for the amoral is whether there's a substantial risk of getting caught.

Beyond the raw act of wrongfully giving money (e.g., bribes) or wrongfully getting money (e.g., kickbacks), the need to cleanse these criminal proceeds is dire, resulting in a high risk of money laundering associated with bread-and-butter organized economic crimes such as drug, firearm, and child pornography distribution. Money laundering is especially difficult to control. Fundamentally, operating an enterprise, obtaining finance for the enterprise, investing discretionary funds of the enterprise in other enterprises—these are routine and lawful activities. Done with criminal proceeds and the same acts become unlawful. Thus, differentiating between lawful monetary transactions and unlawful monetary transactions demands both a great deal of relevant experience and competency on the part of the investigator and a sufficiency of computer-based data readily available for algorithmic testing.

Even so, the adroit criminal record keeper can conceal or omit the attributes providing links to and hints of illicit transactions (e.g., use of unsuspected front companies or straw men). Thus, professional skills in financial services (e.g., lawyers, accountants, bankers), including the use and misuse of wire transfers, are a required part of every successful organized economic crime enterprise.

The most typical form of cooperation in (transnational) organized economic crime groups may be the informal partnership comprised of a few core members aided and abetted by ephemeral relationships resembling employer-employee and independent contractor associations (Von Lampe 2012, 183). This structure of cooperation—a form of compartmentalization of risk of detection by law enforcement—empowers the group, creating persistent and robust relationships that resist easy discovery and dismantling by state actors (Klima, Dorn, and Vander Beken 2011, 24). These underworld partnerships have upperworld offices, but knowledge of the compromised character and real reputation of these professional offices is difficult and expensive to obtain in the globalized informal partnership arrangement. No forms 1065 are filed with the Internal Revenue Services for these associations in fact.

Moreover, recognition of the reality that much discussion, analysis, and rule- and policy-making about the threat of organized crime is not knowledge- or evidence-based but a reflection of budgetary priorities motivated by factors beyond data (Van Duyne and Vander Beken 2009, 279). It's not all about crime-fighting, even organized transnational economic crime however elevated the threat. These ideas suggest that it is important to interpret theories and concepts, as well as the purportedly supporting empirical data, promulgated by officials and generally accepted by experts with a critical eye. The data may be invalid (i.e., not faithfully representing the underlying reality) and not reliable (e.g., assented to and used under a quasi-groupthink consensus process among privileged decision- and policy makers).

Transnational organized economic crime cannot both be the greatest threat to civil society in decades and something that, notwithstanding giving law enforcement agencies oodles of money, results in a scarcity of convictions in practice. It seems the task of reducing the risk of transnational organized economic crime is Sisyphean in nature.

Indeed, the formation, development, redevelopment, and dissolution of organized crime groups is a social phenomenon designed to obtain profit, gain, and influence outside the rule of law, with the caveat that what is deemed organized crime is a matter of official policy and declaration (cf. financial services in support of tax avoidance/evasion). It is changeable, morphing from/to purely illicit cooperation to/from co-optation of the rule of law itself (e.g., corrupt and organized influences over the executive, legislative, and judicial branches). For example, a politician may receive a bribe or campaign contribution—these transactions are cousins.

While there are many similarities between the operations of legitimate and organized crime enterprises, law enforcement cannot fine or otherwise punish organized crime enterprises with the same tools used against legitimate enterprises sponsoring criminal acts. For example, non-prosecution and deferred prosecution agreements are not used against organized crime enterprises as these have no right to exist notwithstanding the legal fiction of the establishment of legitimate enterprises. Thus, organized economic criminals, such as banks behaving badly, may have their sins deferred but this is and was not available to the Gambino crime family. By analogy, this may illustrate the difference between a legal fiction and an unlawful fraud. Ironically, the legal fiction (e.g., a duly incorporated financial services provider in the Cayman Islands) is clearly imaginary, having only legal/official effects, but the unlawful fraud is real, having victims that breathe and bleed.

Importantly, organized crime, while global and local in many respects, is primarily a local phenomenon supplemented and empowered with a vast but transient and impermeable network that often extends offshore to loosely affiliated, semi-autonomous units. However, rigorous and formal collusion and consolidation with other international criminal groups is not the norm (Varese 2012, 249). Consolidated financial reports and tax returns are not issued. Thus, organized crime groups and gangs tend to maintain their own identity and informal social structure as these are the sources and means of their influence. They commit crimes, conceal evidence, and manage the distribution of criminal proceeds through the cooperation of members within the different levels.

Organized crime as a locally determined phenomenon notwithstanding these extensions into venues farther afield has important consequences (Edwards and Gill 2002, 210). The threat is tenuous but real; sinister but hard to observe; changing yet persisting; invisible to most but hyper-visible to law enforcement. Organized crime seems a paradox, with the shadow as presented by conventional law enforcement interpretations as monstrous, but for an overwhelming majority of the public—organized crime is hardly visible.

Cooperation among the criminal nodes of this transnational organized crime matrix, which includes local gangs and facilitating professionals, is transactional more than ethnic. The local origin indicates the nodes' primary source of strength. While support such as offshore financial services and supply chains are essential, these do not transmute the overall and overarching character of organized crime. Whether transnational or regional, organized crime is more likely a federation of regional influences dedicated to the accumulation of financial gain and power in the political economy, licitly and illicitly where necessary, held locally but facilitated globally.

Briefly, bosses and underbosses organize and manage; lieutenants and capos supervise and facilitate; soldiers and associates cooperate and implement on the ground. A rigid structure cannot survive across the hazards presented by rival groups and gangs, and law enforcement targeting as the weakest link(s) can lead to the implosion of the group. Flexibility of network enhances success in a given venture and contributes to persistence through time. The organized crime group or gang at the core of operations functions like a regime of middle managers within an enveloping family of high managerial agents that are loosely affiliated with one another across geographic areas. A friend of a friend goes a long way to extend the reach of organized crime, but this does not make it a global behemoth.

Generally, competitive entities that seek a share of the limited resources within the same political economy generate tension that breeds conflict. Where violent means and fraud are viable tactics, the growth and persistence of organized crime groups are not surprising (Nakamura, Tita, and Krackhardt 2020, 3). Thus, the degrees of freedom contemplated, experienced, and implemented by organized crime groups place it at a competitive advantage without adequate counterintelligence and reliable rule of law delegated to protection of their victim-class, which may as likely include rival gangs as impoverished debtors.

The willingness to use force and threats puts organized crime at the same functional level as the state, which normally reserves a monopoly on the application of force. Organized crime levels the playing field, but its members, associates, and facilitators assume the risk of incarceration. Indeed, organized crime presents a formidable shadow to the state because it will co-opt professionals, politicians, and judges; it will cheat and use violence and threats of violence against those whom it senses strive to disable it. But this is the shadow only, a bad dream. Mostly, organized criminals are more desperate than potent; more crude than sophisticated; more likely to take foolish risks than adopt the safe, conservative course of action. Organized criminals struggle to overcome and transcend their own vulnerabilities, which include the desire to partake of life with a limb or two in the underworld.

CHAPTER 2

Welcome to the Gig (Crime) Economy

The legitimate gig economy liberates employers from having permanent workers, contributing to government-imposed charges such as unemployment insurance and workers' compensation, and they need not obey workplace regulations like minimum wage and overtime laws (Moynihan 2019). It is not hard to see the attractiveness of such a laissez-faire governmental approach for organized crime and black marketeers, especially enhancing the profitability of gray enterprises (i.e., part legitimate and part illegitimate like Enron). The gig transfers much financial risk to the worker-independent contractor from the hirer-principal, which not so much reinvents the relationship between high managerial agents of organized economic crime groups and their underlings, but seems a transfer of the paradigm from organized crime to the legitimate commercial sector. Organized crime groups really have been a gig and not a Fortune 500-modeled enterprise.

Moreover, the use of freelancers like that available in the gig economy dovetails well with the deployment of straw men to facilitate organized crime infiltration of other markets and venues. In brief, the use of straw men is intended to conceal the link to illicit activity and organized crime figures (Woodiwiss 2015b, 91). Straw men and front companies are used to compartmentalize the organized criminal activity, which ranges from opportunity-generating actions to criminal proceeds concealment actions. Each node in the distributed criminal network functions as a material and compartmentalized element in the informal organization and value chain of the illicit enterprise. The gig nature of these relationships within and between the nodes furthers expediency (e.g., parts are more readily replaceable than large collections of parts) and effectiveness (i.e., compartmentalized units are removed from the big picture thinking that could otherwise aid law enforcement upon its discovery of the true nature of any given compartment). The gig is akin to a bankruptcy remote vehicle to isolate business risk in the parts from the whole enterprise or network.

The gig offers opportunity for profit and gain to desperate individuals on a transnational basis. There is no shortage of individuals in (self-perceived) need of increased financial resources and means to live, if not thrive; for example, the population of the desperate well exceeds the availability of fertile financial opportunity. With scarcity comes competition for both legitimate and illegitimate ventures. The desperate are readily exploitable.

Understanding transnational organized crime as a distributed network among gigging individuals, associates, and management of multi-levels and influence is facilitated by grasping that organized crime is a type of wrongdoing within the illicit family of corruption (cf. Varraich 2014, 10–11). Organized crime is not pure at the individual level (e.g., associates may have legitimate occupations); at the entity level (e.g., a legitimate business may front for its illegitimate activities); or at the institutional level (e.g., police, public prosecutors, judges, and legislators may intentionally further organized criminal activities, whether through commission or omission). Globally, the gig extends within and across all these levels. It can do so effectively and efficiently because it is adaptable, opportunistic, untethered to rigid infrastructure and superstructure, and fluid—a criminally disposed matrix changing shape as necessary to infiltrate legitimate businesses, officialdom, and recruit new members with, perhaps, little to lose.

The pool of potential organized crime recruits is innumerably large, and this is not due to an overabundance of evil tendencies in human nature specifically or in society generally. In fact, organized crime is an alluring (informal) occupation due to what it seems to offer: the opportunities for money, power, and related special consideration have long been a part of society, with some individuals gaining much and most not gaining at all. However, organized crime seems to offer those in a hurry a measure of success not otherwise attainable. The mob initially lures not necessarily the preformed and hardened criminal but the malleable criminaloid, who, without a deep and abiding sense of moral sensibility, seeks the faster path toward success notwithstanding the risks (Ross 2007, 44–45; originally published by him in 1907). Whether the mob takes the form of a vertical hierarchy or a horizontal gig, the amorally impatient may follow such a pathway toward profit, gain, and power, however transient.

The gig is represented by operations, structure, and membership not entirely original, that is, nothing new under the sun here with respect to collective action. While the terminology may be distinct (e.g., wise guy in lieu of associate), depending on the particular organized crime entity, the industry of organized criminal enterprises and networks may be approximately modeled with the following attributes:

- Operations: Crimes of terror (e.g., extortion) and financial crimes (e.g., bribery and kickbacks, fraud) are the norm. The operations function under the cover of plausible deniability (cf. Intelligence agency actions). Actions are planned with respect to both effective commission and concealment (at least as to the identities of perpetrators that seek to avoid the rule of law). The routine exercise of illegitimate business planning forms the essential and practical conspiracy or foundational agreement of the illicit enterprise. Objectives and means are corrupt, flowing from an informal, unwritten charter committing the ever-changing collective to extralegal activities.
- Structure: Design and implementation of informal systems of information and communication technologies and means and methods of securing discipline inside and outside of the enterprise are the norm. While there are no auditable internal control procedures and the establishment of books and records will not comply with the Sarbanes-Oxley Act or the U.S. Securities and Exchange Commission requirements, there are methods understood explicitly and implicitly by internal members and external facilitators that provide assurance that compliance in the conspiracies to commit and conceal crimes is not recognized by and disclosed to law enforcement agencies. Secrecy and fraud are predominant control mechanisms.

- Membership: While there are no formal background checks
  implicating dependence on credit rating agencies and the like,
  there are methods of vouching for members. Personal histories are known. Knowledge of character is implied through
  not only personal familiarity but reputation precedes and
  introduces the member. The "I know a guy who knows a guy"
  means of introduction is more common than, for example,
  reliance on the hometown in Italy from which the member's
  family may be observed to originate. The gig economy
  and criminal industry's tentacles extend not only to long
  ago hometowns but new locales with desperate individuals
  striving for opportunity in whatever form.

The gig provides a useful and approximate paradigm for the problem
of organized crime groups. It is empowered by managerialism, an approach
within the political economy that creates privileges in a few and obligations
for many. To be a high managerial agent is to be like a boss of bosses; to be
a middle manager is to be a boss; to be an associate (those that form the
backbone and muscle of the operations) is to be dispensable.

There are those that give commands and those that receive and implement them. However, this does not occur in a context like a monarchy,
a master-slave arrangement, or a publicly filing corporation in the west.
Moreover, the high managerial agents are indeed more like agents than
principals, but they do not report to boards of directors or trustees; they do
not report to super-predator commissions of other high managerial agents.
There is no antitrust problem with organized crime entities operative under
the gig economy model. If any attribute applies commonly up-and-down,
over-and-across these illicit matrices of crime, it is fear of exposure. They
live in overt or covert shame of their own corrupt and fraudulent conduct.

Organized criminal networks have persisted, though the identities of
the participants and leadership change naturally (e.g., death by old age)
and unnaturally (e.g., death by murder). The reasons vary; however, organized crime's ability and willingness to operate with domestic and foreign
governments, as well as obtain cooperation from secretive intelligence
agencies that may view organized crime groups and leaders as assets in
a common goal (e.g., in the U.S. fight against communism), empower

it to make uncommon, unexpected, and undisclosed allies (Marshall 2018, 71). Opportunity for outsized financial gains (e.g., casino operations, licit and illicit) and furtherance of the ideology of private ordering (e.g., capitalism) may be reason enough to sustain both the motivation of joining in the pursuit of unlawful collective action and the motivation of committing to such a life for years. There are no employer-sponsored 401(k) plans in these networks to support retirement. However, there is a form of social capital and bonding that occurs, however temporary and tenuous, among the friends inside and outside of the criminal matrices.

Additionally, there is commonality between traditional, legal corporate and illegal, criminal network structures:

1. The high managerial agents have limited liability. The directors and officers in traditional corporate form have insurance policies, business judgement rules, and the limited liability (not personal liability) created by corporate law for the corporate shell, whereas the high managerial agents of the illicit form have independence from the dirty work of associates—the independent contractors without a formal contract with these high agents. Impunity, whether formalized in the legal corporate structure or informalized in the flexible hierarchy and loose confederation of planners and doers of organized criminal matrices, is the default at the top. Just as the CEO of Uber or Lyft is insulated to a great extent from the bad acts of his or her independent contractor drivers, the leadership of organized crime networks are delinked from the bad acts of the network through lack of written agreements and clear overt acts showing common purpose with the bad doers.

2. In lawful corporate form, the directors and officers defer and hide under the protections afforded to the principal, that is, the corporation. In unlawful criminal associations, in fact the high managerial agents are loyal primarily to the transaction(s). There are no duties of care extended for the benefit of the subordinates, who get little (though it may be substantial for any given transaction) other than the illicit commission. The lawful corporate form and the transaction are principal and the reason for existence of the high managerial agents.

3. The phrase high managerial agent works to identify the separation between thinkers and planners versus the doers with dirty hands. Whereas

the licit high managerial agent can absolve him- or herself of liability and responsibility for actions taken in the corporate name (allegedly for the benefit of the corporation), notwithstanding their effects on the subordinates, the illicit high managerial agent is focused on the transaction(s) and his or her take, notwithstanding its effects on the subordinates.

4. In the licit sphere, a primary objective is to avoid civil liability; in the illicit sphere, a primary objective is to avoid criminal liability. Impunity depends on the erection of an effective shield, whether corporate form or delinked associations. In both sectors, it seems that concrete risk flows downward and high reward rises upward.

It's a gig. It's not meant to last forever in the same form and context within which it arose. That's the point; that's the means of persistence. The gig is remotely linked to the high managerial agents, requiring the skills of criminal investigators and the surveillance techniques of intelligence agencies. The separation between high managerial agents and the underlings gives rise to impunity. The gig is on the line or liable, but the architects and primary beneficiaries, including high agents, are concealed in the labyrinth enabled by high technology and digital currencies.

The unlawful transaction cannot be readily traced from its source or vouched from its effects. Illicit financial flows have origins and beneficiaries obscured by the electronic maze available through the Internet. When law enforcement cannot put a name of attribution (e.g., the Gambino crime family) onto the unlawful schemes, it seems as if they don't occur. The value of the gig is its smallness; its seeming remoteness from anything large and terrifying. This criminal response to American-style law enforcement combatting American-style mafias makes perfect but unfortunate sense.

Importantly, organized economic crime groups function as revolutionary agents against the law and order regime in place. Through gig-structured criminal matrices, their activities undermine the spirit and intent of the laws and regulations as written, yet they proceed independent of any political party or corporate banner. They operate like termites, eating away at the infrastructure and exposing the fecklessness of the superstructure of the political economy. It's no wonder that the American-style response (proactive well-funded application of law enforcement and intelligence agency detective control mechanisms) is heavy-handed.

CHAPTER 3

Why Smaller/More Flexible Cell-Like Nodes and Networks?

While organized crime had been traditionally conceived as a secretive, rigorously structured, top-down controlled organization, the actual unlawful activities may be committed by much smaller groups linked loosely and transiently to larger organizations that covertly assist in providing resources and weapons. There is a downstream and upstream pathway to organized criminal activities, all of which attempt with more or less success in conveying a patina of legitimacy society wide. To be immediately perceived as illicit is to signal ominously to law enforcement agencies.

The tenuous links and pathways may be transnational. There's little real patriotism to organized crime at high levels (cf. profit maximization of legitimate capitalist economic enterprises); there's offshoring. However, this mutual assistance and dependence should not be interpreted to suggest that transnational organized crime is monolithic or a single phenomenon (Migration Policy Institute 2018). This would pose a threat to its very existence and persistence. Moreover, this is not to suggest that transnational organized crime groups are concealing their uniform and monolithic structure and operations; instead, it just does not exist.

The idea of any small group of individuals creating a transnational criminal group operating globally and extralegally would be practicably impossible, given the surveillance tools and financial resources at the beck-and-call of law enforcement and intelligence agencies. (The possibility that one or more influential transnational organized crime groups could have been covertly detected and tolerated with a wink-and-a-nod, for whatever reason, may form the substance of another inquiry ...)

Importantly, organized crime leadership faces challenges from the state (e.g., law enforcement agencies) and competitors (e.g., legitimate commercial enterprises). The ebb and flow of what reaches the attention of the public at large is not really discernible; the public is ignorant, notwithstanding the best of intentions and competence. Recognition and measurement of organized crime are not formally adequately disclosed through crime statistics and otherwise. The problem of organized crime is more analytical than empirical. However, some attributes are beyond reasonable dispute.

Organized crime has been defined as "glocal," local in nature and global in reach, at least with respect to London, which may serve as the "laundry of choice" (Sergi 2018). Criminal activities and proceeds need to be cleansed of the organized crime taint, however imperceptible. This may fairly characterize much of modern day transnational organized crime. Financial centers such as London provide all the necessary professional facilitators and the cleansing network.

For example, Chinese transnational organized crime organizations vary in structure and size, with flexibility and adaptability key to effectiveness (Berry et al. 2003, 1). Opportunism demands loose confederation more than rigid hierarchy, especially where law enforcement and intelligence agency tools and techniques result in broad surveillance of information and communications, which comprise the lifeblood of the act of organizing, whether for legitimate or illicit ends. Organized economic crime as conforming to the ExxonMobil model is (and likely was) more myth than fact; its treasury department cannot be reached via telephone or e-mail. Properly, the focus for understanding organized crime and mitigating its risk lies in apprehending the mechanism of the utilitarian pragmatic network analogous to the contact-making and influence-peddling of commercial (insurance) brokers and/or bundlers in the context of political fundraising. The knowledge and skills of the financial services professionals are indispensable, whether the crimes originate in China, the UK, or the United States.

Flexible and fluid cell-like criminal networks operate under the principles of expediency and convenience, creating a self-protective defense mechanism that does not threaten their reason for existence (Williams 2001, 75). Generally, each of the cells is useful but not essential. No one cell threatens the whole criminal enterprise, and each cell extends its own (illicit) influence across its own patron-client relationships in the political economy: favors are granted and received with informal but real rights and obligations attending these transfers of consideration akin to a creditor-debtor state of affairs without the incriminating documentation of contracts and need for appeals to courts of law or equity.

Organized crime is capitalism on steroids. Socially acceptable capitalism in the United States, for example, offers traditional financing through banks and debtor-creditor relationships mediated by the rule of law. Organized crime transcends these constraints, becoming a hard currency provider for those that cannot use banks and are desperate enough to assume the risk of its range of sanctions (e.g., loss of limb or life) when unable to repay the borrowed currency. In a sense, organized crime is pure in its abandonment of rule of law; in its ability to thrive without state subsidy; in its capacity to generate a range of transactions characterized by dog-eat-dog and vicious relationships, without resort to a legal right of mercy or debt forgiveness. It is this terrible character and cancerous reputation of organized crime that help it to intimidate and succeed, notwithstanding any state's formal position on the matter.

Organized crime could not succeed without desperation among individuals located within its venue and jurisdiction (cf. its glocality).

The criminal networks grounded in the gig economy are not modeled on publicly reporting entities like Lyft and Uber. Enterprises, public and private, licit and illicit, depend on the availability of a pool of unemployed and underemployed individuals seeking pathways of independence. These may appear as opportunities inside and/or outside lawful enterprises. The gigs are impermanent from the perspective of the organized crime associate and the independent contractor driver (or other service provider), but the operations, structure, and forms of membership persist through spacetime using the financial metrics and related rubrics of specialized jargon common in the upperworld of the political economy. Assets and income matter.

In the case of organized crime, the generalized jargon consistent with generally accepted rules of law, accounting, and financial reporting applied in the case of lawful enterprises is not used. There are no periodic audits and reviews, consolidation of financial reports, or segment analyses. The specific gig may be short-lived, but the means and methods of extracting value from customers and victims are long-lived and merged into the asset, income, and equity accounts within the political economy, though not attributed accurately and completely to the entities responsible for the underlying transactions.

The smallness of each gig composes an immaterial element of organized crime, whether measured broadly, locally, or glocally. Multiples of these capillaries facilitate the creation of criminal proceeds; facilitate the washing of these proceeds; facilitate the allocation of these proceeds to leadership, middle management, and rank-and-file alike but not in magnitude. However, there is no paymaster; no finance department; no compliance officers. The paradigm of organized crime as ExxonMobil may close the loop, however, accuracy is sacrificed for convenient (and profitable) myth.

While the focus on smaller networks using a microeconomics (or similar) approach toward measuring and mitigating the effects of organized crime groups is not altogether novel, it tends not to address threats such as elite fraud and grand corruption. There is no Mr. Big, but not all organized crime individuals are equal. The use of data warehousing (e.g., the collection and examination of suspicious activity reports) and network analysis (e.g., the study of disclosed patterns among beneficial owners) techniques may be more effective in detecting some surface-level transnational organized crime than in discovering high-level cooperation among leaders in the affected political economies (Levi 2012, 47). An analytically useful and broader methodology that investigates not only agency and individual actions at the lower levels in organized crime groups but investigates the leadership in structuring the global pathways of organized crime, including often attendant political corruption and organizational fraud, could uncover heretofore ignored facilitation processes.

The venues and jurisdictions of offshore finance are commonly known by financial intelligence units. However, there is a structural impairment of attribution: the financial institutions housing the accounts may be known, but the account details are inadequate at best, fraudulent or non existent at worst. What is lacking is the competency to group accurately and completely the distributions from the accounts. The beneficiaries' relationships with the ultimate controllers need development.

Analysis inclusive of the biases resulting from uneven data collection across jurisdictions and shifting legislative and executive priorities of law enforcement and regulation would be helpful. Who prioritizes, makes, and enforces the laws should be examined with quantitative techniques (e.g., regression analysis) and qualitative tools (e.g., *qui bono*), though, of course, these methods are not mutually exclusive. Together, these analytical methods might reveal the underlying global and structural dynamics that explain why and how organized crime groups have transformed into gig-like operations. Likely, such an approach, if undertaken independently, impartially, and with adequate resources, would reveal transnational organized crime groups as a political problem with national security implications (Naim 2012, 101). The gig-like nature of organized crime allows it to hide and resurface without detection.

Indeed, the organization and operation of criminal groups, whether conceived as a limited joint venture or continuing illicit enterprise, present risks to property (e.g., theft by deception), person (e.g., extortion), and state (e.g., terroristic activity). Assessment of the risks posed by organized crime groups are not limited to persons in their individual capacity but extended to states (and corporations) in their governance capacity (Choi 2014). From the perspective of the target, whether the custodian of tangible property or bureaucrat vested with state secrets, the vulnerabilities of the guardian or security system, especially those dependent on the integrity and due diligence of humans (cf. automated systems of control), are subject to exploitation by organizations of criminals (more so than by an independent, rogue individual).

Gig-like infiltration may be barely or even entirely unnoticeable by the state's surveillance system. Victims at high levels can disguise transactions more effectively (e.g., contributions and not bribes) than victims at low levels, who are unlikely to receive the official attention required to remediate the threat. Gig-like infiltration may be fast and fluid, exploiting the targets' vulnerabilities as opportunistic contingent assets.

Thus, the gig-like cellular structure resembles the old school neighborhood (traditional) theory and conceptualizing about organized crime groups, except the former is looser and flexible where the latter is grounded and fixed. The cell replaces the neighborhood, and the gig substitutes for the method. There is less commitment to the physical neighborhood and much exploitation of technology and cyber-connections. However, in whatever form the organized crime group is operationalized, the specialized function of the pursuit of profit, gain, and influence outside (but sometimes drawing upon) the rule of law is the overarching attribute (Lombardo 2013a, 34). Thus, the neighborhood is expanded through high tech information and communications technology; the hard currencies are converted into electronic liquid flowing from shore-to-offshore-to-shore accounts for use in obtaining hard assets (e.g., real estate).

The need for social and community proximity is displaced in part by the information and communications technology. Moreover, the nature of the gig commitment shrinks to short-term over long-term capacity to pursue fairly immediate profits, gains, and influence notwithstanding the rules of law. After all, the long-term is only a series of short-terms, manageable through gig development, dissolution, and redevelopment.

The organized criminals need not be neighbors to collude: social distance has been bridged through virtual (computer-based) linking among individuals, locally-, regionally-, and internationally based, resulting in a matrix more similar to terrorist cells than neighborhood social clubs. This is an attribute providing immeasurable strength and opportunity for growth; for capacity to change and adapt; for the ability to hide and lie dormant.

Moreover, the initiation and build-up of organized crime groups survive the threat and breakdown imposed by law enforcement and other means due to the facility of forming cells inside and outside of neighborhood and jurisdictional borders. Simply, the cell provides a superior structure, though not without its own risks, including the ability to vet the required competency skills face-to-face.

However, the desperate character of those who knowingly enter the domain of organized crime groups has its own control mechanism. These individuals are familiar with the reputation of the high managerial agents of organized crime; they are also cognizant of the occasionally brutal character of those implementing the desires of the managing agents. They assume the risk.

CHAPTER 4

The Criminogenic Network and Role of Legitimate Financial Institutions

Organized crime is transnational in many material respects. The complexity and accessibility of the international financial system, including the deposit, transfer, and exchange of currencies for or with U.S. dollars, lends itself to concealment of the sources and uses of financial funds (Central Intelligence Agency 2008). Based on the estimates developed in 2009, at least 2.7 percent of global gross domestic product (GDP), equivalent to $1.6 trillion, of available criminal proceeds are laundered, with only an estimated 0.2 percent of such laundered proceeds seized and frozen by law enforcement (i.e., the interception rate) (United Nations Office on Drugs and Crime 2011, 7). These statistics suggest an enormous problem not adequately mitigated by financial institutions' anti-money laundering tools and processes, and public sector regulators and law enforcement agencies charged with supervising and monitoring financial institutions.

Additionally, supply chains (e.g., sources of drugs, firearms, and humans for trafficking) are internationalized. Export-import is the rule. Distribution and logistical chains use all the traditional pathways (e.g., by air; by rail; by waterway; by road) called upon by legitimate commercial enterprises. The transactional circuit of organized crime (i.e., money to illicit goods and services to money) is akin to legitimate commerce; this empowers the attribute of organized crime concealment.

In fact, the bank secrecy regimes effective in many jurisdictions of the United States and the UK may be the primary pathways for money laundering notwithstanding self-promotion and hifalutin language by high government officials. The incentives to launder from the perspective of the financial institutions are great—much greater than a commitment to a robust enforcement and regulatory infrastructure that would negatively affect the capacity of the financial institutions' highest priorities: (1) having control over money; (2) maintaining confidentiality between the institution and its customer (Young and Woodiwiss 2020, 23–24). In a sense, the problem of organized crime control via inspection and oversight over financial institutions and self-regulation has failed, with the role of the U.S. dollar and the exploitation of the U.S. and UK criminal law policies essential to preserving the ill-gotten capital of organized crime group leadership and the financial well-being of financial institutions. Money laundering may be mutually beneficial for financial institution and organized crime agents.

Conceptualizing the problem of global money laundering as a failure of domestic and international collaboration among financial intelligence units and the financial institutions, while seemingly incontrovertible, pays inadequate attention to the root cause. A symbiotic relationship between lawbreaker and custodian is not solvable as a problem of collaboration; it is a problem of misaligned interests and incentives. Impartial and independent inspection and oversight would seem to provide a more effective paradigm than a proposed global self-monitor of transactions among financial institutions.

As overseen by the U.S. Department of the Treasury's Financial Crimes Enforcement Network (FinCEN), special measures may be required of financial institutions to address the risks of global money laundering. These focus on transaction analyses, beneficial ownership information, and conduit and correspondent accounts (U.S. Department of the Treasury 2011). The effectiveness of these measures is questionable, though the desirability of their adoption is a step toward remediation of the problem. Policy and law effectiveness are often evaluation based on criteria such as enforcement actions such that when enforcement actions increase the problem is purportedly en route to solution, but when enforcement actions decrease, the problem is prematurely deemed solved. This is a sort of "heads I win, tails you lose" evaluation process.

A better measure of progress would be to set up a system wherein all offshore transactions are accurately, completely, and timely registered under an independent, impartial audit or inspector general investigative global regime. This would generate significant, if not fatal, opposition due to, among other things, powerful preferences of the economic elite to preserve secrecy and liquidity of financial funds.

For example, the global nature not only of operating organized crime groups (i.e., conducting illicit sales of goods and services such as drugs, firearms, and gambling) but of investing in products such as privately issued bonds supported by the income from, among other sources, organized criminal activities, is readily demonstrable (Johnson 2020a). This mainstreaming of profit-seeking and passive (unearned) income maximation may fairly be deemed a distressing attribute of modern capital investment and finance. Capital seeks growth and protection independent of national borders.

Indeed, there is serious concern in the U.S. law enforcement about the underlying purposes, motivations, and effects of large investments in private equity and hedge funds (Lloyd 2020). Their usefulness for money laundering is due primarily to the large investments (e.g., millions of dollars is not unusual) and to their overall opacity (i.e., disclosure regimes are not robust in political economies such as the United States). The process of flows and stores of financial funds is intended to be covert and private—not transparent and supportive of any particular public interest.

Money laundering may be interpreted as a key mechanism in obtaining practice use of criminal proceeds (often) free of their unlawful origins. While the term money laundering is pejorative and the conduct is usually illegal under many jurisdictions, the predicate acts—creating financial transfers to and from dark venues and secretive jurisdictions—are not avoided by those with enough savings to justify the transaction costs. The ability to avoid taxation transforms an ordinary return on investment to alpha growth, the stuff of hedge, and private equity funds' reason for existence.

Perhaps, the root of the organized crime and financial institution problem may be understood upon recognition that on the banks' balance sheets, no distinction is made between lawfully and illicitly sourced funds (Raab 1984). If only dirty money were really muddy, slimy, and stinky… However, cash deposits comprise an essential ingredient of profitability for banks (and other commercial institutions), so there are explicit and implicit incentives to look the other way or at least not look too deeply into the depositors' money-generating enterprises. With cost disincentives impairing the commitment and capacity of institutional compliance, whether internally within proprietary control systems or externally situated in independent contractor and regulatory regimes of inspection and oversight, and financial benefit incentives turbocharging amorality, if not immorality and indifference to rule of law, through focuses on share price, earnings per share, and accompanying bonuses for senior management, transnational organized economic crime has the unacknowledged structural advantage in the dominant political economies (e.g., the United States.).

Financial institutions may grease the wheels of legitimate commerce, but they also support the growth of illegitimate transactions. At heart, there is a conflict between the financial institutions' need for profitability, gain, and influence and the publics' need for protection from social harms incident to money laundering (e.g., loss of tax base supporting public expenditures, capital outflows). The proprietary network, especially where their elite constituents' influence over public policy is great and the potential opposition is dispersed and unorganized, trumps the required real commitment to public inspection and oversight to control (illicit) financial flows.

CHAPTER 5

Overview of the Size of the Problem

It is difficult to identify and estimate the problem of organized crime. Politics has suffused the subject matter (Critchley 2009, 234). While public prosecutors proudly proclaim and publicize their purportedly high-profile convictions of organized crime bosses and underbosses, the public may not perceive any material difference in their immediate attendant circumstances, that is, organized crime may seem almost invisible to most residents before and after the much-ballyhooed official enforcement actions. Contrast this perception with the hypervisibility of social and individual problems implicating, for example, drug abuse (e.g., opioid addictions). Thus, the effects of organized economic crime are experienced widely throughout society both before and after reportedly momentous enforcement action (e.g., convictions of NYC crime family bosses).

Just as illicit financial flows accompany the lightly regulated global stream of electronic money transfers, the distribution of organized crime's fruits (e.g., drugs, firearms, political corruption) continues seemingly unaffected. The enforcement action is more theater than remediation. One may fairly question the real efficacy of headlines proclaiming yet another high-level mafia crime family boss/underboss takedown—the overall flow of illicit goods and services remains untouched. Obviously, the boss is not really as influential as publicly proclaimed by law enforcement press releases. The illicit games continue.

The conception of organized economic crime as paramilitary groups suggests that legally impairing the freedom of the generals and admirals will cause the armies and navies to implode. In reality, the size of the problem is largely unaffected by the legal decapitation of the titular head created by law enforcement hand-in-glove with mass media. Good press is easy for some; good outcomes—way more difficult to achieve, measure, and preserve.

By defining the problem as one originating with a few bad and powerful actors at the top of rogue hierarchies of criminal activities, the publicity-seeking and reputation-inflating leadership in the political economy may claim victory when the evil pariahs are undone. However, even this strategy is Sisyphean: note that like triumphs in the global war against terror where disablement of the latest and greatest threat to freedom and democracy occurs with fair regularity only to be immediately followed with the rise of yet another latest and greatest threat, so is the war against organized crime. Powerful bad actors seem to pop up like mushrooms in a forest after a rainstorm.

Not only is the magnitude of the problem not accurately and completely measured but the direction and trend of the problem are likewise opaque. High level math cannot create relevant and reliable models of the vector of organized economic crime where the underlying data are materially deficient. In a sense, policy-makers' and law enforcement agencies' assumptions and estimates may be fairly characterized as self-serving, imaginary statements unmoored with the realities experienced by individuals whose lives are impaired by the persistent drug and firearms distribution problems.

Moreover, the new organized economic crime is transnational (cf. global), engaged in illicit networks composed of associations of small cells of individuals with extensive distribution and concealment schemes requiring innumerable individuals. A link analysis showing these intertwining and overlapping relationships across the globe would comprise an awe-inspiring figure or graphic, but such a representation would disclose more chaos than complexity. It materially lacks predictive power and truth value. However, these associations in fact, whether legally formed or informally coordinated, involve the following types of criminality (see National Security Council 2011):

- Corruption of state institutions, including bribery
- Corruption of markets, including intellectual property theft
- Cybercrime, including wire fraud
- Terrorism, including illicit financial flows
- Trafficking in drugs, humans, and weapons across land, sea, and air, including through unguarded and unauthorized ports of entry

As defined above, the size of the problem is immense, suggesting that, perhaps, the proliferation and persistence of transnational organized economic crime is not a bug but a feature of the modern global political economy (at least as depicted in the west). To the extent these depictions are intentionally used to support other agendas (e.g., American-style imperialism) may be the subject of another's research.

Estimating the extent and gravity of organized crime influence is clearly difficult. As in the UK, where fraud is the most commonly experienced crime (National Crime Agency 2019, 43), organized economic crime covers a wide range of criminal conduct: from drugs to firearms to other schemes for profit, gain, and power, a shared material element of these actions is concealment. Offenders do not strive to be apprehended. Focused and persistent efforts toward uncovering organized economic crime are necessary for both justice and measurement. These efforts may be inconsistent, varying with the public priorities of the period under examination. Times, policies, and priorities change. Commitments are ephemeral.

Deception methods are key in executing successfully (at least, from the offenders' perspective) both organized and individual criminal activities. From commission of the predicate acts forming the offense to concealment of the inculpatory evidence of the crimes to conversion of the proceeds from criminal activities, the tactic of deceit is common and necessary, including the use of physical disguises (e.g., masks), activity disguises (e.g., routine service provider), and diversions (e.g., outside disturbance to refocus attention of the target's guardians) (Lafleur, Purvis, and Roesler 2015, 42–43).

Of course, wherever the art and techniques of deception are invaluable and highly rewarded, they recur more frequently and with increasing sophistication. This further obfuscates the size of the problem. Opacity is the norm.

Moreover, deception may enable the offenders to avoid brute force and physical violence, as well as to hide their identities. Analogous to making an audit trail byzantine and labyrinthine, the methodology of offender deception tends to leverage the offenders' ability to commit criminal activities without meaningful attribution by law enforcement and witnesses, taking advantage of the pre existing deficient knowledge base of those outside the criminal network. The markets of criminal activities, criminals, and criminaloids are vast and not enumerated in any census counts or reliable statistical techniques. Hide-and-seek is especially effective where law enforcement cannot identify the movers-and-shakers in the network; knowledge of any given participant is too remote from the core because there is no core. There is a vast web of connections and pathways.

The United States faces threats from transnational organized crime that, while also difficult to measure, are likely significant and will persist (Office of the Director of National Intelligence 2018, 13–14). The hidden and pernicious entanglement of fraud as specialized economic crime with general transnational organized economic crime contributes both to the failure to uncover the existence of organized economic crime groups and their roles, means, methods, and persistence in transnational transactions (Police Foundation and Perpetuity Research 2017, 25).

By way of example, the so-called tri-border area extending from Puerto Iguazu in Argentina to Ciudad del Este, Paraguay, and to Foz do Iguacu, Brazil may comprise the largest illicit economy in the west (Brown 2009). Now, the globalization and interdependence among organized criminals (and terrorists) from disparate countries in the world cannot be denied absent willful ignorance. This phenomenon grew from the seeds of organized criminal activities in local venues. The growth may fairly be deemed malignant, and the locations forming the original roots of organized crime are distributed throughout the globe.

The profit, gain, and influence opportunities are too great. Organized economic crime is transactional activity that will provide alpha returns, so long as one is practiced in the art of deception. Ironically, without the rule of law making organized economic crime a prohibited class of transactions, the return on investment would likely be significantly reduced via competition. As it is, few want to compete in the markets of organized criminals, and any form of intra-market competition may be lessened through arrangements common in the antitrust domain (e.g., bid rigging, price fixing, customer allocation, market manipulation) such that the competition among organized economic crime groups does not rise to a highly noticeable level (e.g., that which would alert law enforcement and regulatory authorities that a major social problem exists). In a sense, the criminal markets are more self-regulated than commonly believed.

Internecine turf battles observed in drug trafficking are usually local-ized and fairly simple to resolve (e.g., murder, mayhem, intimidation). The so-called mafia wars are overblown, especially when examined from the top-down perspective. The leadership has too much to lose, but the rank-and-file, with much to gain, is more tempted to engage in local acts of rivalrous violence.

Upon recognition and appreciation of the clandestine, corrupting and corrupted, and essentially fraudulent nature of tales originating about organized crime influence, the scholar and analyst face enormous difficulty in measuring accurately and disclosing precisely what it is that sometimes generates a moral panic from what it is that is more an appar-ent threat that abruptly fades from public consciousness. Empirically, one cannot identify sufficient competent evidence of the ebb and flow of organized economic crime independently of mass media pronounce-ments and law enforcement boastings (or oversights). Organized crime is modernity's sinister bogeyman and evil shapeshifter (until it becomes a low law enforcement/intelligence agency priority like the period post-9/11 in the United States). They fade like low density meteorites. The half-life of organized economic crime incidence and persistence is beyond objec-tive measurement, and inter-subjective measurements proffered by those with an axe to grind (e.g., public prosecutors seeking career advancement, journalists seek fame and fortune, cooperating witnesses, and informants seeking leniency). The biases obfuscate, yet a careful observer cannot help but notice that the goods and services of organized economic criminal activities (e.g., drugs, firearms, child pornography, human trafficking) show no significant level of shrinkage notwithstanding the dissolution of conceived threats such as New York City's five families.

Organized economic crime influences have historical bases (e.g., the *yakuza* in Japan) and modern interpretations (e.g., *la cosa nostra* or the mafia in Italy and the United States). For example, research in the UK suggests that the threat of organized crime is dwarfed by the resources arrayed against it, and other reasons may exist for presenting organized crime as a high risk to society (Sproat 2012, 328). After all, careers may be developed and leveraged into other opportunities under an exagger-ated response to a problem not deserving of such attention and resources. The "tough on crime" attitude properly disseminated through the mass media may result in the garnishment of significant influence in the political economy beyond any given law enforcement agency and into society at large (e.g., high political office, richly compensated consultant). That is, these tough crimefighters, whether as politicians or law enforcement agents, parlay this attitude into oversized influence, exploiting fear and vulnerabilities nurtured in the public at large by the policymakers and law enforcers.

Organized crime is fairly definable, however, inaccurately and incompletely. That is, the crimes can be catalogued (e.g., extortion, drug smuggling, human trafficking, firearms distribution) and counted (e.g., surveys of administrative jurisdictions with official data and public prosecutors with aggregation of cases data), but the overarching or undergirding organized crime group is more like a floating signifier. It means whatever the law enforcement agencies and public prosecutors say, it means. There are insurmountable measurement errors at play.

Consideration should be given as to the preparation of an accurate and complete database built on intercepted and indexed communications (e.g., U.S. National Security Agency sweeps). If the information within every communication carried through wire, through mail, and through wireless were not only gathered but reliably interpreted and catalogued for parallel investigation by law enforcement agencies (e.g., U.S. Federal Bureau of Investigation) and disseminated timely and transparently to the public at large, the threat assessment of organized crime would be conceived with equitable accuracy. Perhaps, there's more to be gained by the elite decisionmakers within the political economy to maintain the secrecy of this information. A threat based on ignorance may be inflated and deflated at will, depending on the effectiveness of propaganda methods and psychological operations (psyops); or maybe it's just an over-abiding commitment to the civil and constitutional rights of the public at large.

Briefly, organized economic crime persists and grows as a global, national, regional, and local set of phenomena due to common weaknesses in formal (e.g., governmental) approaches to solve the problem of organized economic crime. Enforcement of laws is irregular across jurisdictions, consistency and design of rules of law describing and prohibiting the predicate and enterprise criminal activities differ across jurisdictions, and inadequate data exist to capture the breadth and depth of the causes and consequences of organized crime (Council on Foreign Relations 2013). With measurement error characterizing efforts to define the set of problems contributing to and resulting from trans-jurisdictional crime, the theoretical and conceptual framework for understanding organized crime itself may create further issues. Problems ill-defined are not properly solved.

Neither self-serving overestimation (e.g., by public prosecutors, politicians, criminal investigators) nor naive underestimation (e.g., by the same sets of professionals!) of transnational (and local) organized economic crime help to address the risks presented by organized crime. Moreover, the clandestine nature of organized crime suggests that it may be a problem more suitable for mitigation by intelligence agencies than law enforcement agencies, assuming the threat rises to the level of national security concern.

Of course, due consideration should be extended to the logical and empirical difficulties of calibrating the level of threat where so much profit, gain, and influence can be obtained via manipulation of the threat level. Here, the conduct of legitimate and illegitimate collectives of social actors intersect within the political economy. Whereas scale may be estimated fairly reasonably by measures such as market capitalization in the legitimate domain, these measures generally lack applicability in the illegitimate domain. Nonetheless, the overarching goals are similar in appearance and shared in function:

1. Profit – both domains seek operating profit; that is, an enterprise or entity that sustains itself through routine and repeated conduct (e.g., distributing goods and services on a regular basis, engaging in tax avoidance/evasion schemes).

2. Gain – both domains seek (capital) gains; that is, engaging in non-routine transactions that increase the economic and financial viability of the enterprise or entity (e.g., property and casualty loss claims, real estate exchanges, bankruptcy liquidations) in one-off commercial activities.

3. Influence – both domains seek to preserve their power in the political economy through developing and nurturing special relationships with other (external) actors that create opportunities for further commercial activities (e.g., political campaign contributions, lobbying).

Thus, where the legitimate enterprise pursues objectives in conformance with the goals (e.g., selling lawful goods and services in the market), the illegitimate enterprise's objectives are comprised of pursuits within the gray and black markets (e.g., selling stolen pharmaceuticals, selling unlawful drugs and other contraband).

Whereas the size of the legitimate enterprise is estimated through the issuance of regular financial reports, which may be independently audited, the size of the illegitimate enterprise remains in the shadows, subject to inflation and deflation according to the tenor of the times and the agendas of the leadership in the political economy. Should ordinary residents be terrified of organized crime? It depends on whether the resident borrows money from the neighborhood shylock he or she cannot pay back; on whether the resident gambles on the losing end with bets placed with the local unregistered bookie; on whether the resident transacts in illegal drugs, unlawfully distributed firearms, or engages in human trafficking …

It may be fairer to conclude that one's greatest risks are found in mundane activities that have little to do with organized crime (e.g., driving a vehicle recklessly; engaging on the disfavored end of office politics; abusing lawfully prescribed pain medications, etc.).

CHAPTER 6

Traditional Organized Crime (e.g., Mafia)

Traditionally, organized crime (e.g., the mafia or *cosa nostra*) was comprised of an opportunistic crime syndicate (Hortis and Jacobs 2014, 180). In a sense it still is, like white-collar crime and street crimes generally. Specifically, organized economic crime exploits pre existing opportunity structures where the rewards are likely and worthwhile, and the risks are practicably ignorable. This is the traditional perspective of organized crime groups strategically exploiting existing opportunities through fairly rigid top-down structures of command-and-control. In this sense, it resembles many legitimate commercial entities.

However, there are competing theories (cf. the emergent perspective whereby organized criminals proactively create opportunity structures) (Silverstone 2011, 193). Thus, the function and operation of a criminal network with nodes and tentacles extending into diverse goods and services across wide expanses of geography serves as a modern paradigm. Previously, it might have taken a village to organize a bank heist; presently, it takes a global consortium to develop the foundations of plans (e.g., deploying the skills of information technology experts pejoratively known as hackers), to coordinate through the use of inside knowledge (e.g., a conspiracy of criminal associate and employee of the victim) the optimal time and place to execute illicit plans, and to conceal and wash the criminal proceeds (e.g., professionals of offshore banking). This is not your mom-and-pop or local crime family in action.

Moreover, while stealing a little can readily be accomplished independently, stealing much may demand collusion inside and outside of the targeted victim(s). Human beings as social animals are predisposed to cooperative ventures, licit and illicit; human beings also seem predisposed to take orders, which suggests the usefulness of command-and-control structures and top-down hierarchies of bosses and associates following the chain of command. The organized crime group as the Gambino crime family directed and controlled by the godfather made sense, superficially. Moreover, who was to disagree publicly? Not the megalomaniac leadership of illicit collectives; not the career-advancing, super-crimefighter of public prosecutor and criminal investigator. This paradigm of organized crime collectives offered much to many. But what about truthfulness; was this more mythology than evidence-based?

The traditional conception of organized crime as a vertical, rigid command-and-control enterprise based on ethnic background (e.g., Sicilian-style mafia in Palermo morphing into American-style mafia New York City) makes a great story. This illicit collective purportedly enjoyed and featured a brotherhood based on origins of birth and ethnic ties. Thus, it was not class-based but a construct in which, for example, any Italian tracing his/her (but overwhelmingly his) ancestry to Sicily, Naples, Calabria, and so on would be eligible by this identity trait to become a made member or associate, regardless of the humbleness of one's birth and upbringing. It was a unit dedicated to illicit collective action, but it did not discriminate on the basis of socio economic background, according to the myth.

Compare the quaint interpretation of the illicit ethnic brotherhood with the professionalization of organized economic crime where sophisticated lawyers, bankers, accountants, and so on are necessary to create both the appearance of legitimacy and the availability of laundered criminal proceeds. Traditional organized crime has been modified by the professional managerial class of finance, insurance, and real estate because these sectors capture high net worth individuals' financial and economic interests (cf. the economic elite) and, as importantly, preserve and grow these interests. The safety and confidentiality of financial flows, licit and illicit, depend on the knowledge and skills of the investor, portfolio manager, and facilitator class (not a collective characterized by many low-borne and humbly raised individuals, and as importantly, not restricted or defined by the identity trait of ethnicity).

Organized crime may be conceptualized from the perspective of its groups (e.g., mafia families, street gangs) or its markets (e.g., illicit drug distribution, illicit firearms distribution). Theoretically, while these may be two different ways of identifying the problem, they are not either/or pathways. In fact, organized crime persists and thrives along transnational horizontal and vertical lines (United Nations Office on Drugs and Crime 2010, 18). Because the markets are gray and white, they are inseparable from their market participants. That is, organized crime is comprised of numerous, if not innumerable, players operating in upper- and under-worlds. It is collusive in nature, global in effect. Moreover, it is more anonymous than notorious. To be a public figure (e.g., Gambino, Gotti) is to attract the attentions of law enforcement agencies and industry regu-lators: one cannot demonstrably dwell in the underworld and obtain, for example, a casino license.

In fact, making a hullabaloo of the specific prosecution of semi-public figures such as John Gotti, Jr., while likely furthering the public pros-ecutor's careers, does not cause a material adverse effect on organized economic crime, generally. This comprises an imaginary solution to an ill-defined problem.

Importantly, the practice of individuals in the employment of organi-zations to coordinate and cooperate with other individuals in the employ-ment of other organizations in the furtherance of criminal activity is not unique (e.g., O'Brien 2019). That individuals organize is to be expected; that individuals commit crimes resulting from these organizations is not surprising. That the organized crime group would be represented as a shadowy enterprise mirroring the largest corporations in the west is surprising.

If one appreciates the fact that traditionally, depicting organized crime like ExxonMobil allows the myth-creators to partake in a seemingly noble exercise: powerful, evil criminals are imprisoned—please give me my political plum (e.g., judgeship, high elected office, high appointed office) and anoint me as a hero. The American crime-busters of the 1960s, 70s, and 80s needed these myths to parley their role in controlling a develop-ing political economy (viz., the United States) to greater heights of their own profit, gain, and influence. Under this fact-pattern and dynamic—never define a problem such that it cannot be solved by yours truly.

Jurisdictionally, not all organized criminal activity is investigated and prosecuted as organized economic crime (e.g., securities fraud may not form the basis for private party civil enforcement of the racketeer influenced and corrupt organizations act, Henning 2018). Thus, a lay definition of organized crime would likely include many more cases than a legal expert's definition of organized crime, notwithstanding the presence of organization (e.g., conspiracy), membership in an enterprise (e.g., employee), which is used to facilitate the unlawful obtaining of profit, gain, or power such as insider-trading schemes, market manipulation, price-fixing, bid-rigging, customer allocation, and lobbying, to name a few.

The mafia does not have a monopoly on organized crime: The state does through what it outlaws and prosecutes; through its influence over mass media; through its exploitation of the vulnerable and uninformed public at large. For example, New Jersey state criminal investigators ominously raised the threat of a particular motorcycle gang in New Jersey through publication in a popular mass media news outlet in New Jersey on what can fairly be deemed slim empirical data or evidence supporting this alarm (Napoliello 2020). Critical questioning and impartial assessment of the state investigators' report was not evidenced. This was and is not unusual reporting.

Whether actions compose the material elements of a crime depend on the influences at work in the specific political economy defining the crime. In practice, these forces may also significantly influence enforcement of the crime. State action (e.g., criminal investigations, public prosecutions) does not occur in a vacuum, and crimes, including organized economic crime, are the result of commitments of state actors to conduct preliminary and full investigations, as appropriate, and follow up on these actions, where necessary, through the office of the relevant public prosecutor. Without recognition of the vital role played by the state in defining what is and what is not organized crime, measurement of this criminal activity may be materially and unqualifiedly understated.

In brief, it's way easier to posit organized crime as a comparatively small group of Italian or Italian-American thugs exercising an exaggerated deleterious influence on the lives of resident victims, notwithstanding that most of these purported victims have no clue they are even victims (excluding obvious victims in some cases like extortion). The ultimate question is who has committed the greater fraud—the myth weavers presenting as gospel the traditional organized crime narratives; the criminal justice actors taking the public and its purse for a long, expensive ride; or the so-called white-collar fraudsters (e.g., Skilling at Enron, Ebbers at WorldCom) bamboozling investors, employees, and pensioners?

If the actions of the U.S. legislature were to be considered a signal of formal federal government interest in the problem of organized crime, the period between 1934 and 2003 would comprise the focus and hey-day of its published transcripts of hearings (Von Lampe n.d.). However, due to the evolving nature of organized crime, federal enforcement tools and adequacy of federal resources dedicated to the mitigation of the risks posed by organized crime persist as major public safety concerns (Finklea 2010, 25–26). The problem as conceived originally as a collective of bad individuals of shared ethnicity does not provide adequate guidance currently. Without endeavoring to disprove the preeminence and potency of small groups of illicit directors (e.g., the crime commission—panel of boss of bosses) and illicit officers (e.g., bosses of families), since such exaggerations of influence cannot be disproven and need not be disproven presently as the concern in this work product is the nature and threat of organized transnational economic crime and not whatever inheritances exist from collectives such as the five families of New York City. What was inherited might have become legitimate. However, what remains is something altogether different from the Gambino crime family or American-style of traditional organized crime.

Both the desire for outsized profits perceived as available from orga-nized criminal activities and the desire to use terrorism financed through organized criminal activities together present potentially grave economic and bodily harm threats to the general welfare of the public at large. Just as the cell-like nature of terrorism transplanted from venue to venue does not leave telltale indicia in many cases, the gig-like nature of organized economic crime morphs across geographies, united by the conditions nec-essary to get away with major crimes. These crimes are more horizontally brokered than orchestrated vertically.

Ironically, the enterprises most like traditional organized crime groups, many of which failed to survive the criminal justice purges of the 1970s, 80s, and early 90s in the United States, would be those oper-ating in the financial services sector. They are regulated and registered, but they are allowed to conceal formally their clients' and their own transactions, checked, if at all, by public auditors paid and controlled to a significant extent by these financial services companies. Regulation, especially in the major financial centers such as London and New York City, tends to be light. Apart from bureaucratic registration—a control that neither prevents nor detects major crimes—the financial services industries, including fintech such as Wirecard, traverse the globe, enhancing the liquidity and secrecy of electronic stores and flows of financial funds (i.e., e-money).

While American-style enforcement has focused on the enterprise characteristic of organized crime groups (cf. the conspiracy element separate and apart from the requirement of a continuing criminal business), a characteristic developed in the 70s and applied in the 80s in the United States that had resulted in disabling financial sanctions and long terms of imprisonment for some bad actors and associations—in fact, some independent scholars have focused on more limited definitions of organized crime groups, preferring to demand certain characteristics be found in the underlying criminal activities such as direct and fixed control over production and distribution of illicit goods and services (Leukfeldt, Lavorgna, and Kleemans 2017, 296). This would seem to exclude much of what passes for gig organized economic crime networks as described in this manuscript. However, such an approach does not give due account for the innovative capacities of organized criminals and modern information and communications technologies, that is, there is little net value in seeking to obtain criminal monopolies (e.g., exclusivity over the dark web) and hegemony over the multi-step supply and logistics chain (e.g., adoption of the parent-subsidiary relationships common in many legitimate global organizations). The criminal liability exposure is too great.

Additionally, the pool of desperation is not of rigid dimension and unvarying volume. The gig enables transcendence of the traditional crime family, outsourcing criminal liability and making remote any demonstrable connections of the parts to one another. The web of organized criminality is expedient, impermanent, and without stars and kings. Through anonymity, the effectiveness of the criminal web is enhanced. It moves and reforms with the breezes of opportunity. Moreover, opportunity is a global construct.

The advantages of flexibility and variability in procuring and delivering illicit goods and services include making detection and punishment more unlikely and administratively difficult. Charging an individual with operating a global and significant criminal enterprise, if the evidence were developed, is an easy sell to criminal investigators and public prosecutors. Charging end-users and apparently bit players—not a great sell. This variability conceals comparative influence. There is no vertical command-and-control fact pattern against which to assess the illicit market participants' role. The players seem useful for any given transaction but not necessary to the enterprise as a whole; of course, this may likely be owing to the absence of an enterprise. Indeed, there are a series of illicit transactions, but these are difficult to source against any one individual or collective. There are no directors and officers (but this is not to conclude that a strict equality and unyielding horizontality exists among all participants; some are more equal than others).

Contrarily, the five families of New York City-based organized crime groups in the 20th century were too hidebound to New York City venues and vulnerable to enveloping federal jurisdiction and rules of law such that the Racketeer Influenced and Corrupt Organization Act's (RICO) generous, at least from the state's and later plaintiffs' bar perspectives, criminal and civil powers were applied to substantially emasculate the bosses and underbosses of these traditional organized crime (American-style derived from Sicilian-style) groups. In effect, the kings and princes were taken out, leaving innumerable associates to ply their unlawful trades through other means, methods, and crime scripts.

The success prosecutions of American-style, traditional organized crime leaders demonstrated to the underworld that acting like an industry mogul in expensive suits and luxury cars is only a short-term strategy. More discretion and distribution of criminal and civil risks are required. It became practical to broker illicit transactions and obtain significant profits, gains, and influence without owning the underlying goods or providing directly the underlying services. Better to take an illicit commission off the top of the (criminal) proceeds than to take the gross and exercise managerial control over the distribution of the gross. Who needs the gross if you can get the net up front?

CHAPTER 7

Historical Overview: A Few Key Concepts

The intent of this manuscript is not to detail dates and moments of organized crime infamy. Who got murdered in whose barbershop while eating what Italian pastry is of little moment, presently. History is not so much for the remembrance of key dates and acts, but for the identification and memory of key patterns and attributes that persist. Thus, this overview functions more as a survey than a complete recitation of organized crime groups everywhere. After a few instances of conduct, murder is a bad ending; extortion is the power of intimidation and force; fraud is a clever way to steal; organizing to profit, gain, and influence—how is this a surprise? Some don't obey the rule of law, especially where they think they will get away with it—does this shock the conscience? Organized criminals and their groups, tight or loose, pretty much function like one another (let me count how many ways I may steal from thee …).

Organized crime is neither a new nor a necessary phenomenon. Its occurrence, growth, persistence, and decay are contingent on social factors within the political economy, that is, as an organized activity, it needs cooperation and trust among members; as a crime, it needs the formal superstructure legislating and defining that which is criminal. Moreover, it needs to be enforced and counted; otherwise, organized crime would officially be nil.

While the roots of organized economic crime are understandable as a byproduct of disharmony within the society and the desire to secede from the social, market, and legal norms by which most others in the political economy abide, these roots do not necessarily lead to the trees and branches of organized economic crime. Sometimes, disaffection and alienation lead to despair unaccompanied by organized economic crime; something else happens to generate the cancer of (transnational) organized economic crime. There are catalysts.

Thus, it is important to distinguish between mediator variables, which explain how organized economic crime occurs, grows, and persists, from moderator variables, which explain the increase, decrease, or stasis in the levels of organized economic crime. Beyond the obvious circumstances (e.g., needing a jurisdiction that defines, enforces, and counts that which comprises organized economic crime), the jurisdiction at risk needs a pool of desperate individuals of a critical mass. These would-be offenders believe organized economic crime is their most viable option. This is not so much rational choice as exclusion from real opportunity. Of course, the wealthy in assets and the richly compensated by income cannot credibly be viewed as lacking real opportunity as much as lacking integrity, a moral compass, and concern for others. At a minimum, the desperate and the narcissist provide a potential pool of informal candidates for organized economic crime.

However, attendant circumstances vary, and so does the motivation for participating in organized economic crime. For example, the numerous employees of Wells Fargo bank that agreed to create customer accounts out of thin air to meet quotas and bonus targets were a bit desperate, a bit compromised morally, a bit shortsighted in attitude, and so on. The important point is that this is not a rational choice. If given fairly equal opportunity and largely equivalent return on investment of effort and cost pathways, few would choose the pathway of organized economic crime. It's less rational choice than perception of no real choice in the matter, perhaps.

A society and attendant political economic wherein organized economic crime is rampant (and this applies to organized economic crime in fact and not organized economic crime as measured by criminal convictions and other manipulable proxies of the criminal justice system) is a society in decay and despair—where individuals of ill will have captured too much of the state.

Generally, when organized economic crime is discussed and analyzed, the dependent variable usually becomes the rate of organized crime over a given period. Thus, no convictions, no problem. In a significant part, this is due to the failure of the state to properly catalogue organized economic crime, preferring measures that focus more on street and property crimes (e.g., extortion, theft) and less on reportedly legitimate actors behaving badly (e.g., financial institution employees' and their agents' misconduct, consultants' misconduct). Also, there's no shortage of a colorful history of American-style mafia wrongdoing, including murders. Pardon the borrowing of an old saw, but "if it bleeds, it leads."

Knowledge and understanding of the New York City mafia is nonetheless important, even if overstated and overextended. Real people were murdered; actual property was taken and extorted; illicit drugs and other contraband were distributed. Black and gray markets existed and exist, the New York City five families got more than their fair share. But it's not just the American-style mafia that is relevant toward understanding organized crime groups as both a dependent variable (though preferably not measured exclusively in accord with official crime statistics) and an independent variable that causes inimical changes in the host society. The New York City crime families showed what brute force and intimidation are capable of producing and taking.

Moreover, there have been a multiplicity of officially recognized formidable traditional organized crime groups. These include the Italian mafias (viz., the Sicilian *cosa nostra*; the Calabrian *'ndrangheta*; the Neapolitan *camorra*), the American *cosa nostras*, the Japanese *yakuza*, and the Russian mafias (Sergi 2020, 184). These groups are depicted with conceptions and theories similar to the American-style organized crime networks. Like the New York City mafia, they are subcultures within the home political economy, which may be contrasted with the so-called emerging (transnational) organized crime groups that exploit new vulnerabilities (e.g., cyberspace) in the modern political economy. Their roots are not as deep into the past like the traditional organized crime groups. However, this distinction in typology is not mutually exclusive in relation to the criminal activities, that is, both forms of organized crime groups may engage in similar unlawful conduct (e.g., drug and firearms trafficking).

Three concepts are clear:

1. Organized crime has a longstanding tradition of operating domestically and internationally. It's not new.
2. Organized crime groups should not be limited to those constructs depicting personalism and the big man syndrome (e.g., the Gambino crime family). That's old school and not terribly relevant currently.

3. Organized economic crime groups, especially those that operate globally, pose an underappreciated threat that may dwarf the risks presented by organized crime groups.

Importantly, recognizing that organized crime is a species of corruption within society is essential notwithstanding the conventional narratives about traditional and emerging organized crime groups or even more modern theories depicting the nouveau bugaboo referred to transnational organized crime groups. As with corruption generally, organized crime is a symptom of the governance dynamics and institutional qualities at work (U.K. Department of International Development 2015, 79). In brief, a global economy implies extended access and additional opportunities for organized crime groups that have the technology to connect directly or indirectly with associates and independent contractors internationally.

Also important is the recognition that organized crime groups are more *ad hoc* than standing. Mostly, they exist for the job and not the career. The worker bees are more like informal contract employees (cf. the gig) than members of a permanent workforce, which gives weight to the elevation of the overall threat. However, pinpointing its key nodes and controlling persons is difficult, if not illusory, absent significant power to intercept and catalogue domestic and international communications (cf. the U.S. National Security Agency).

Determining causes for preexisting organized crime groups like the Italian mafias or the American-style mafia such as that formerly dominant in New York City, conventionally known as five crime families and commonly referred to as traditional organized crime, as well as so-called emerging organized crime in the form of transnational groups is difficult due to the opacity of the criminal markets. While highly specific tests and observational data may be used, including quantitative regression analysis of panel data comprised of convictions per capita over many years, the tests are not sensitive to all the organized criminal activities, charged or not. Moreover, the tests are characterized by the intellectual risk of allowing for too many false negatives; that a criminal justice system has not investigated and prosecuted conduct as organized crime does not support the inference that organized crime thereby does not occur. The lens' focus of interpretation and inference is too narrow. This is an especially noteworthy and troublesome risk in consideration of the presence and persistence of organized economic crime, whether transnational or local.

Sound analysis cannot abide materially inaccurate and incomplete data and evidence.

Nonetheless, a panel of experts concluded that notwithstanding the disparate local and regional characteristics of organized crime centers and nodes, certain findings are likely persuasively supported:

1. There is not likely a significant specialized attribute to traditional organized crime. It operates like a conglomerate with multiple product and service lines (e.g., gambling, prostitution, retailing drugs).
2. There is likely a significant specialized attribute to emerging (transnational) organized crime. It operates within limited product and service lines (e.g., trafficking sex workers, manufacture and wholesale distribution of drugs, trafficking in undocumented workers).
3. There is likely significant overlap between traditional and transnational organized crime with respect to transportation services (i.e., logistics) (Finckenauer and Chin 2004, 25–26).

The picture created by snowballing through scholars' and practitioners' analyses is that of a complexity of organized criminal activities, sometimes specialized and opportunistic, sometimes generalized and semi-permanent, that is difficult to apprehend using the taxonomy of traditional, emerging, and transnational. The markets are black and gray; the underlying conduct is rarely transparent but for the occasional investigation and conviction whereby the defendants' and witnesses' testimonies need to be carefully and skeptically inquired of due to the attendant circumstances, including state actor careerism and bad actor exchanges of evidence favorable to the state for leniency.

The depiction of organized white-collar crime (e.g., financial institution "mis-selling") as something separate and apart from organized economic crime, whether resulting in formal charges or not, goes beyond traditionally conceived ideas and measures of organized economic crime. Perhaps, with the recent law enforcement agency focus on transnational criminal activities will arise a more enlightened and logically consistent approach that interprets organized crime as corruption of markets (cf. antitrust law) and not merely a collective of desperate individuals of shared ethnicity. The problem goes way beyond the Russian mob.

While organized crime seems a market-based problem (i.e., the informal creation of alternative venues for goods and services, licit and illicit), this does not necessary imply that the proper unit of analysis for organized crime is entity- or enterprise-based. It is the organic creation, expansion, contraction, and change in shape of the network or web that comprises an indivisible context (e.g., field embedding the conduct), superstructure (e.g., distributed decision making), and infrastructure (e.g., information and communications technology) for organized criminal activities.

Within the data presently, the biases are systematic. They are not easily remediable, and they are not reliably quantifiable. Inaccuracy and incompleteness may need to be surmounted with other analytical methods that take conventional narrative with the proverbial grain of salt. This is not to deny the historical existence of the Gambino crime family but to properly weigh it in revised context (i.e., an incident to a lightly regulated political economy). Alternatively, one may accept and tolerate conventional narratives, overblown threats, and ignored social harms. Life as an ostrich (is for the birds!).

These arguments are not intended to prove that there is an equality of return on investment for all organized criminals. However, there is no big man. The most useful and poignant question to be asked under this line of inquiry is how do organized crime groups operate symbiotically with presumed legitimate commercial enterprises (e.g., answered in part by reference to the facilitators)? How do illicit sources of income and wealth contribute to the riches of the richest? Much opacity here, with the abiding presumption of legitimacy attaching to the wealthiest, notwithstanding the absence of any forensic audit having been conducted against the assets and income streams of these well-positioned individuals. Presumably, they are extraordinarily wealthy because of their smarts ...

CHAPTER 8

Japan (i.e., Yakuza)

The predominant organized crime group in Japan is the *yamaguchi-gumi*, commonly known as the yakuza. It has been described as a highly centralized and structured organization, resembling legitimate businesses with its hierarchy. In fact, the Japanese government's approach to the yakuza is to regulate it and not ban it outright. It operates in the open, and membership in the organization is not inherently illegal (Matsangou 2017). Thus, the yakuza is to the Italian mafia what cigarettes are to hashish (as evaluated under the U.S. norms and law).

Moreover, interpreting the yakuza as a single organization would be misleading. Instead, it is comprised of many smaller organized crime groups and gangs whose actions are licit, illicit, and hybrid. The enterprise of yakuza is more plural than singular; more heterogeneous than homogenous; more process than structure; more dispersed than concentrated. It is indeed an exemplar of organized economic crime.

However, organizations begin, with their origins usually recessed into centuries-old folklore that cannot be investigated absent the willingness to pursue a doctorate with pre existing knowledge of the functional language, these organizations, illicit and licit, adapt or perish. The yakuza persist, though like the so-called five mafia families in the New York City metropolitan area, they are not now what they were represented to be from the narratives propounded by criminal investigators, public prosecutors, and scholars.

Reportedly originally developing in the early 18th century (if not earlier), the yakuza were not materially different from modern mafia groups, specializing in protection rackets, gambling, and other fraudulent and illicit conduct (Szczepanski 2019). The forms of criminal activities are familiar, still practiced today in Japan and elsewhere.

One questionable attribute is important to consider, that is, are the entities currently described as organized crime groups innovators or imitators? Echoes of organized crime are not Italian, Sicilian, American, or sourced entirely from any one ethnicity; these patterns reverberate through time and across geography. The yakuza filled and presently fill a niche—the gap between actions that get initiated, authorized, and completed through official means such as the government and actions that satisfy needs and wants beyond (or quicker than) the capacity of official organs of supply and demand.

The premium that one incurs by subjecting him- or herself to the vagaries of organized criminals cannot be measured macroeconomically. It may be disclosed as the vigorish to obtain a loan from a loan shark; the cost of obtaining pharmaceuticals of unsure origin and quality in the gray market; the long-term price to be paid by obtaining a business partner via the illicit pathway. This premium would also include as a cost of doing business the sanctions imminent for failure to live up to the informal, legally unenforceable agreement (e.g., death, grievous bodily injury, arson, insurance fraud).

Thus, only the desperate need apply for the assistance of organized crime groups; this is as much a Japanese issue as a New York City issue as a Sicilian issue. Cf. victims of organized economic criminals operating through valid licenses and registrations in various jurisdictions—these individuals may not even realize they are being bamboozled, made to overpay, in receipt of counterfeit goods. The global economy is not too remote from America's wild, wild west.

To an extent and degree neither accurately nor completely captured by current data gathering tools and techniques but communicated from generation-to-generation across cultures through formal and informal narratives, whether in Asia or North America, organized crime persists as a cause and effect within the society at large and political economy as a whole. Yakuza members beginning with the social status of outcasts and losers in the 11th century, as individuals in the Burakumin caste, persisted until becoming over generations charitable, valued contributors in modern day Japan, only to face an abundance of new laws designed to enfeeble their organizations. Adapt or perish applies at the individual and entity levels. This is a familiar trajectory: failure turns to success then deals with an existential threat from law and public policy (Oliver 2019). Consider the reputed influence of New York City's five families—only to be undone by the harsh sanctions of the racketeer influenced and corrupt organization act in the 1970s, 80s, and 90s.

Brute force characterizes the original attribute and lever of success; that is, the capacity to use violence to obtain financial and other resources from an inadequately protected victim or even one's lower ranked associates and colleagues seeking illicit advantage is and was indispensable. This, of course, comprised a low bar of entry to the illicit profession. Extortion may be the mother action of entities like the yakuza, providing libraries and media with terrifying stories and mythologies of days gone by. However, there's not enough economic and political growth in those original seeds. Its power dissipated. Thus, the yakuza adapted to the opportunities presented to white-collar criminals, initiating and exploiting pathways of wider development beyond the locality of the neighborhood and into a wider realm of commerce. From importing drugs to fixing construction contracts, the yakuza methodology and practices seemed familiar to Western perspectives.

Observations and analysis of organized crime groups in Japan are supportive of the theory that organized crime groups develop from fecklessness of state institutions, that is, the organized crime group provides an alternative to state-provided and state-sponsored rights enforcement mechanisms (Milhaupt and West 2000, 92). Thus, organized crime groups may operate under weak state jurisdictions as a protection racket (and not merely as the traditionally conceived extortion racket and purveyors of prohibited products and services such as illegal drug distribution, prostitution, and gambling): counterintuitively, organized crime groups may enhance overall justice in the state albeit through informal and illicit means. The real issue is what is meant by justice, with offenders, victims, rivals, criminal investigators, and so on possessing different opinions. The state in reserving the creation and legitimation of markets to itself; in reserving the right to commit violence against residents and others to itself; in establishing protocols and processes (transaction costs) before authorizing action; in substantially delimiting the right of self-help of the residents—has unwittingly given rise to the practical need for organized criminals to exist. Like other organized crime groups, the yakuza live in neighborhoods and may attend to neighbors' needs where the state is too slow or obtuse.

The amorality of organized criminals lends itself to flexibility of role. However, need someone to give a beating; need some cocaine; need sex with children; need unregistered firearms; need to curry favor with a judge, jury, or politician? Organized crime steps in where the state won't. As organized crime goes global, the connection between manufacturer, distributor, buyer, facilitator, bank custodian … becomes tenuous. Not knowing the victims of human trafficking, or the dead from drug over-dosing, or the lifeless bodies taken down by the use of firearms, the organized criminal is remote to his or her effects. However, this does not interfere sometimes with being a good neighbor.

Organized crime groups played a similar role in Italy, especially in Sicily in the late 19th century. Even the bad guys take off their black hats on occasion.

CHAPTER 9

Italy (e.g., La Cosa Nostra)

Organized crime has been conceived as originating from regions in Italy, including Calabria, Naples, Sicily, and so on. Investigators have mapped out networks demonstrating the centrality and concentration of mafia-linked firms, with the construction industry as a key commercial locus of illicit structured groups of criminals. Thus, in Sicily, at least, organized crime groups are linked to one another via counterparty and associated financial transactions. Emerging technology from the arXiv (2014). This is not especially surprising as construction provides the opportunity for a significant level of financial extortion (e.g., paying for protection and other parasitic conduct) involving trades with fairly low barriers to entry (e.g., masons, laborers), and the island of Sicily is a fairly small geographic unit.

While some organization is necessary for effective coordination among various sources or earners in furtherance of illicitly extracting financial resources from victimized economic actors, the tendency to overstate the spread and influence of any given network should be minimized. After all, law enforcement and public prosecutors have long celebrated inflicting death knells to organized crime upon the arrest and conviction of mafia moguls, yet the underlying criminal activity persists; that is, the levels of drug, firearms, human trafficking, and so on cannot be described as permanently mitigated upon such outcomes accomplished by law enforcement.

Whether one begins with the so-called Sicilian mafia in the late 19th century or the present perception of the organized crime pandemic denoted as transnational organized crime, it seems clear that organized crime is a comparative function of opportunity: not enough in the licit sphere, and too much in the illicit sphere. Where the potential for large profits and high margins exist, organized crime surfaces. Add political insecurity and weak rule of law and organized crime may flourish

(Dimico, Isopi, and Olsson 2017, 1113). Then and now organized crime may provide, whether summoned by the victim or imposed on him or her, protection like corrupted insurance.

One may fairly question from whom the victim needs protection: The illicit business of extorting protection monies may be stimulated by threats from within the organized crime structure itself (e.g., pay us or else we will impair your ability to conduct lawful business) or outside the extorting criminal structure (e.g., this is a perilous venue, and rival gangs may interfere with the business). The conditions of late 19th century Sicily were characterized by a lack of remedies available in the political economy for legitimate business operators. The mob filled a void. Moreover, this organized criminal activity might have furthered the public interest where the public sector was feckless.

Presently, the void filled by references to the mafia, especially the Italian- or Sicilian- derived species of organized crime groups, may owe its origins to an exaggerated fear and elevated anxiety blown out of proportion by journalists, governmental investigation committees, law enforcement officers, and public prosecutors using platforms principally in the United States to create a devil out of incidents of crime loosely organized but falling far short of a national or transnational threat. After all, it takes a brilliant criminal investigator and public prosecutor to convict a criminal mastermind; lesser criminal convictions do not establish one's bona fides (Albini 1993, 249).

The variable of motivation of criminal investigators and public prosecutors is largely omitted from most historical studies, including those emanating from organized crimes in Sicily, as the data are sparse. In this void, an extravagant (Hollywood) narrative has taken space, transforming myth into truth, without empirical evidence or reliable data.

Of course, Italy and Sicily have not cornered the markets of organized crime. Neither notorious jurisdiction have repressed the development of organized crime groups based on other ethnicities (e.g., gangs of Chinese ethnicities, mafia-like organizations in Nigeria). The sources of organized crime cannot be exclusively traced to Italy and Sicily (Del Monte, Riva, and Vergine 2020). Smuggling people, trafficking drugs, and distributing counterfeit goods are profitable enterprises whether one is restricted tightly to the rule of law or covertly disregards it. Making distinctions based on ethnicities in the analysis of organized crime groups may make a blockbuster Hollywood movie (e.g., *The Godfather*) but does little to further what is essential and persistent about organized crime from what is contingent and convenient.

Then, as now, organized crime has infiltrated many legitimate commercial sectors, including agriculture and food services, pharmaceuticals and medical equipment, road construction and maintenance, funeral services, cleaning services, and waste disposal. Presently, vulnerabilities in the financial services sector have opened a pathway for organized criminal activities (INTERPOL 2020). In many material respects, globalization of high technology and digital work process flows have contributed to the exploitation of the financial services sector, which offers remote services and potentially high value transactions as a lure for the seasoned organized criminal with access to facilitators and co-conspirators such as computer hackers.

While opportunities may preexist for a given organized economic crime group, opportunities may also be created by a given organized economic crime group. In reality, the markets, licit and illicit, are volatile and comprised often of a series of fluid collaborations (Hobbs 2012, 261). The dental practice may exploit financially the opportunity for revenues and reimbursements from a patient's insurance company based on the insurance plan (e.g., two routine services per year), and the practice may create additional financial opportunity based on the plan (e.g., provide inadequate service necessitating more frequent uncovered services payable by the patient). Thus, the dental practice, an organized hierarchical economic unit composed of three or more persons, earns revenue licitly and fraudulently. Conceivably, the practice operating in such a fraudulent manner with six or more individuals may be deemed a continuing criminal enterprise. That this is rarely done so by criminal investigators and public prosecutors speaks to the mismeasurement of organized criminal activity in the political economy, including erroneous analyses about Italy, Sicily, and the United States, among others.

CHAPTER 10

United States (e.g., Al Capone, the "Five Families")

Traditional organized crime folklore posits the five families' (viz., individually, the Gambino, Lucchese, Colombo, Bonanno, and Genovese networks) influence predominating in New York City since 1931, depicting a highly coordinated and integrated system of allocation of illicit financial flows from criminal activities; this superstructure was substantially enervated by the so-called Commission case of 1986 (Raab 2019). However, during the mafia or *la cosa nostra* peak era of the 1960s, the business of organized crime as mediated through the five families in New York City, was thought impregnable due to inadequate criminal laws not sufficiently extended in scope of application and severity of punishment. There was no effective, pervasive, sustained law enforcement criminalizing the organization of individuals for the purpose of obtaining illicit economic gains and power through the instrument of the illicit enterprise in and of itself (separate and apart from conspiracy charges and predicate criminal activities such as bribery and kickbacks). Additionally, supported by corrupt public officials and the creative talents of lawyers and accountants, the enterprise of organized crime persisted notwithstanding changes in leadership (Cressey 1969, 90).

By way of memorializing specific instances of mob influence in New York City from 1968 through 1973, the following observations are provided:

- Some have considered the 1960s to contain the heyday of the five families' illicit control in New York City (cf. Anglen 2019). While the peaks and valleys of mafia control and influence are difficult to measure accurately, the 1960s of New York City and other geographies in the United States offered many opportunities for lawful and unlawful economic exploitation. The United States was the unquestioned economic leader, and New York City was the financial capital of the world. Financial flows, licit and illicit, could be directed and siphoned by those with muscle, whether originating on the streets like brute extortion or from legitimate industries like the record business.

- Traditionally, the organized crime families in New York City, aka *la cosa nostra* (LCN), are five in number (viz., Bonanno, Colombo, Genovese, Gambino, and Lucchese) and have exercised significant influence in the region (and others) since the 1920s, persisting to this day with apparently reduced influence. The LCN is notorious for infiltrating businesses and governments (i.e., bridging the upper- and underworlds) (Albanese and Reichel 2014, 32).

- Moreover, local law enforcement was not consistently an effective deterrent to organized criminal activity (Holland 2019). The strong guardians necessary to protect the vulnerable from organized criminal exploitation were not in place in NYC during this period. Even as late as 1968, little was really known about the inner workings of the mob, and it was not until the early 1970s that some law enforcement actions began to have a noticeable effect on the influence of organized crime (Baud n.d.).

- Also problematic was the infrequency of media attention dating from early conceptions of organized crime dissemi-nated in the mass media in describing criminal conduct in Chicago. In fact, the *New York Times* beginning during the late 1960s through the mid-1980s rarely covered the concept of organized crime; largely, it was invisible (Von Lampe 2001, 100). Thus, knowing about the reality of organized crime was not an empirical concern absent the conceptual framework within which to account for and measure it. The independent reality of organized crime was not empirically, systematically, and rationally investigated and presented to the public at large as a coherent conceptual framework. Organized crime has structure (e.g., bureaucracy with horizontal and vertical dimensions), means and methods (e.g., extortion, murder), and specific goals and objectives (e.g., profit and power).

- Talented musicians such as Jimi Hendrix would comprise an essential part of the mafia's supply chain and profit center. The method of operation was to control income-producing properties where vulnerabilities combined with profit margins made the industry an opportunity in the particular venue. Musicians starting out in NYC were often inexperienced, and access to distribution of the product (e.g., live performances at clubs) was directed and controlled by collectives of corrupt individuals using graft and related corrupt schemes.

- In brief, the general form of the illicit so-called payola transactions was cash from the record company to the independent promoter (later, the artist) to the radio station program directors, that is, this was payola. Sometimes, assets other than cash was exchanged by the promoter to the program director (e.g., drugs, prostitutes) (Byron 1990, 11).

- A related form of payola was comprised of independent promoters affiliated with organized crime who would obtain cash not only from record companies but from illegal operations such as narcotics trafficking, forming a network from which payments would be issued to radio station program directors as payola to promote specific artists' recordings (Holden 1990). Joseph Isgro (though acquitted but associated with the Gambino crime family) was federally charged in 1989 of using this form of payola (Weinstein 1989).

- Allegations of links between organized crime and the music industry are not new, including accusations against CBS Records of having an illicit drugs-cash-extortion racket with members of the Genovese crime family (e.g., Anthony Fat Tony Salerno and Pasquale Falcone) in New York City (Lichtenstein 1974).

- Bootlegging (pirating or counterfeiting) recordings have long been a significant source of revenue for organized crime dating from the 1970s, if not earlier (Holloway 2002).

- As late as the 1980s, the music industry, including players or would-be players in New York City, was allegedly dominated by organized crime (Barron 2014).
- By 1976, the Gambino crime family led by Carlo Gambino was allegedly among the powerful criminal organizations in the United States and New York City (Gold 2019).
- Carlo Gambino significantly influenced the construction and trucking industries in New York City, as well as the unions that controlled the supply of building materials into New York City. He was a partner with casino magnate Meyer Lanksy, who held significant offshore financial interests, including in the Bahamas and Cuba (Schladebeck 2016). Thus, legitimate businesses in New York City were vulnerable to mob extortion at the front end through a variety of pathways such as construction and redevelopment of real estate, requiring not only building materials but the cooperation of truckers bringing the materials to the construction site, which, of course, would include the delivery of supplies necessary for daily operations of businesses. Moreover, the mob's grip on the waste hauling business would adversely impact businesses on the back end.
- A dispersed workforce was and is vulnerable to exploitation by organized groups, criminal and lawful (Jacobs and Project Muse 2006, 256). The music industry was and is populated with individual musicians or small groups that may not be (or have been) inadequately protected and are vulnerable to overreaching and exploitative efforts by organized criminals, including promoters, managers, and others in the supply chain. The guardians did not include law enforcement agencies generally, popular culture, and the mainstream press as the individuals comprising these sectors were absent from any stimuli to enforcement action. It was not a recognized problem. Moreover, the so-called private guardians (e.g., lawyers, accountants, company formation agents, promoters, agents, managers, and so on) were not always adherents of professional ethics and the letter and spirit of the law.

- The music industry during the 1960s (and later) was also exploited by organized crime. The Genovese family and partner in crime Morris (Moishe) Levy, aka the "Godfather of Rock and Roll," were known for assisting eager young talent only to control the copyrights and royalties of their recordings. The rags to riches to rags to drug overdose story like that of Frankie Lymon, who died in 1968, is notorious. Levy died in 1990 (Sucher 2014).

- Other musicians such as Jimi Hendrix fell into a series of troublesome relationships with managers and promoters, including individuals such as Michael Jeffrey, whose integrity and network of connections inside and outside of the music industry have been subjected to debate. Indeed, the profile of Hendrix's business issues have been characterized as a legal and accounting nightmare unresolved to date (Fricke 1992). Artists seeking fame and riches without the protection of a traditional network of lawyers and accountants were and are vulnerable to the predation of organized crime. Allegations against Jeffrey for misdirecting the receipts of income earned by Hendrix into a shady tax shelter in the Bahamas (viz., the Yameta account) are still unexplained under traditional conceptions of legitimate promotion and management activities (Wells 2009, 5).

- Broadly, organized crime (including the Gambino and Genovese families) had exercised a significant pernicious racketeering influence in New York City during the 1960s, adversely affecting the construction, garbage, and music industries (Finckenauer 2007).

- However, if one event could separate and summarize the material differences between the effectiveness of the mafia in relation to the commission and power of organized crime in the 1960s and prior periods versus the 1970s and later, it would be the enactment of the federal RICO Act in 1970 (History 2019). Combining legal powers with the federal Wiretap Act enacted in 1968 and formalizing the legal process of obtaining electronic communications for use in courts and

administrative proceedings, the legal context became prepared
for the challenges with intrusive criminal investigative
techniques and punishing prosecutorial powers (Justice
Information Sharing 2013).

- Together, RICO and the Wiretap Act empowered and
facilitated federal law enforcement agencies in their efforts to
control and prosecute organized crime networks, presenting
both a higher likelihood of detection and a severer range of
punishment (e.g., prison terms, fines) to organized crime
figures. Thus, the strategies and tactics of organized crime
pre-1970s had to adapt or perish under the harsher federal
criminal law enforcement regime.

The series of anecdotes, data points, and observations noted above
provide a sketch of the background of the political economy and state
action necessary to understand how it is that criminal activities generally associated with organized crime (e.g., drugs, firearms and human
trafficking, counterfeit goods) occurred then and now, largely unabated,
notwithstanding the debilitation of mafia moguls and their crime families. Specifically, can globally distributed (transnational) criminal activities occur without directors, officers, and commissioners of the purported
stature and reputed influences of the Gambinos, Luccheses, and so on?

Overview of Transnational Organized Crime

The seriousness and formal conceptualization of the problem of transnational organized crime may be observed in the United Nations adoption of a series of legal instruments (treaties) beginning with resolution
55/25 in November 2000 (United Nations Office on Drugs and Crime
2018). Wrongful conduct, including trafficking in persons, smuggling
of migrants by land, sea, and air, and trafficking in firearms and ammu-
nition, became recognized as an issue that required the intervention
of nations, that is, no one nation could independently remedy these
harmful acts.

The widely encompassing concept of transnational organized crime
developed from decades of actual case studies, criminal investigations,

and public prosecutions implicating numerous crimes and domestic and international jurisdictions. Both criminal and civil sanctions have been implemented (see FBI n.d.). In brief, the nature and impact of transnational organized crime implicate more than one country (Albanese 2012, 1). From the perspective of organized criminals, this makes some sense as the jurisdictions may be divided and avoided, and the race to the regulatory bottom may be pursued.

Discussion and analysis of transnational organized crime requires not only consideration of historical practices contributing to the quantification of risk (e.g., quasi-frequency analytics) but the persistent motivation—profit-seeking by licit and/or illicit means (Rosenblum, Bjelopera, and Finklea 2013, 8). Thus, profit is seen as the primary motivation, making organized crime part and parcel of the market, albeit black and gray. Of course, development of reliable statistics on transnational crime rates and trends is difficult.

Moreover, transnational organized crime is comprised of amorphous, cross-national, and adaptable networks (White 2016, 89). Whether discussion focuses on, for example, Latin American cartels (e.g., Sinaloa cartel based in Mexico) or the financing of terrorism (e.g., the Islamic Revolutionary Guard Corps based in Iran), the global nature of the organization is essential for its success as cash proceeds need offshore laundering both to conceal their source (e.g., drug trafficking) and to hide their use (e.g., firearms trafficking). The financial resources (i.e., funds) flow into and out of correspondent and depositary banks under shell companies and straw men without positive identification of the beneficial owners and real account controllers. In fact, the underlying transactions comprising transnational organized crime are largely hidden as private, confidential, and proprietary information.

The differences in motivation (e.g., to impair the influence of the target government in the case of the terrorist organization; to realize and secrete revenues and profits from trafficking in illicit services/goods), while relevant to the design and implementation of governmental and social controls to inhibit such unlawful conduct, are secondary for the purpose of this manuscript to the shared means and methods deployed to succeed clandestinely in obtaining and using funds. The key criminal objective is to obtain much profit, gain, and influence, which may be evidenced by the control, albeit often covert, of pools of financial resources distributed in domestic (e.g., Delaware, United States) and offshore havens (e.g., Cayman Islands).

Like realization of domestic organized crimes, the means and methods of transnational organized crime are shadowy and based in intransparent networks (e.g., the dark web). Without the big man (e.g., Gambino), against whom the focus of wrongdoing may be affixed, there seems no one person to hold legally responsible, notwithstanding the arrests, prosecutions, and convictions of numerous individuals from South and North America, Asia, Europe, Africa, and so on. Transnational means wider and more frequent criminal opportunity, and with the advent of sophisticated and powerful information and communications technology funds and messages may be delivered rapid-fire across the globe among individuals who may or may not know one another. The impersonal nature of transnational organized crime reduces its vulnerability, as a whole, to law enforcement agencies, though a cooperative of intelligence agencies has significantly more tools to develop the foundational evidence for parallel criminal investigations (Office of the Director of National Intelligence 2020). Of course, this formal power housed in transnational governmental (and likely non governmental, too) secretive agencies pose threats to civil liberties, privacy, confidentiality, governmental sovereignty of target nations, and so on that may dwarf the gravity of threat created by transnational organized crime. For example, the spying apparatus may be used to thwart transparency of governmental and sponsored operations that are inimical to the public interests of not only the hosting nation, but obviously the targeted nations too.

Just as a given domestic legal authority may overstate the gravity and extension of the threat of locally based organized crime, such an authority may disseminate similar messages to the public at large, domestic and international, to justify or excuse other agendas (e.g., imperialism).

As noted above, transnational operations take advantage of, if not actively create, a race to the regulatory bottom. Organized crime organizations and gangs adapt to these conditions and make contacts and extend their networks to wherever they can operate without high inherent risk to their assets, income streams, and special relationships of influence (e.g., compromised politicians and business moguls). Technology and digital currencies have made the globe a situs of opportunity, licit and illicit.

Parenthetically, the efforts to combat transnational organized criminal activities through such means and methods as the deployment of the powers of partnerships such as the Five Eyes has made the world a hotbed of opportunity for extortion. Whether via obtaining evidence of bad conduct of politically exposed persons such as participation in sexual activities with children or use of tax havens to secrete funds embezzled or diverted from the public treasury, the intelligence agencies may have the goods to fight organized crime with (s)extortion. What goes around, comes around; karma can be brutal and vengeful.

Also, the development of transnational organized crime is, in a sense, a natural corollary to the growth of transnational organized economic crime committed by lawfully established corporations (e.g., externalizing the social harms of pollution, exporting of dangerous or tainted medications, exporting of firearms to foment insurrections). To the opportunist, criminal, criminaloid, and law-abider, it's like having a bigger playground.

Overall, perspective and humility are needed in properly conceiving of and theorizing about transnational organized crime. After all, American-style organized crime has been traced more or less to Sicilian-style organized crime, both of which were preceded by Japanese-style organized crime. Really, it's always been a transnational problem.

CHAPTER 11

Notes on Ontology of Organized Crime

Organized crime exists in the political economy, whether analyzed locally, regionally, or globally. Due to specific state-related factors that allow its parasitic influence to grow extralegally and cross-border, organized crime is a species of social pestilence, primarily benefiting a few ruthless individuals steeped in anarchy while harming or presenting a significant risk of harm to almost everyone else it contacts.

In brief, state actors may fail to prevent flourishment of organized crime for numerous reasons (e.g., state actors may benefit financially and professionally from the specific definition and contours of the problem commonly known as organized crime), allowing its power both to expand and to concentrate unchecked (Dudley 2016). Thus, organized crime effectiveness in opportunity generation, profit taking, and exercise of power and influence within the political economy is linked to corruption found in state actors. They may ignore, partake in, or even significantly influence state action normally considered as tools to combat organized crime (e.g., criminal investigations, public prosecutions). The largely intransparent discretion held by the high managerial agents of the criminal justice system may inspire loyalty and good feelings among those who can trust without verification, but any serious endeavor to know the bases for the decisions and robust context underlying the formal decision of proceed or not will likely be frustrated by assertions of privilege and immunity emanating from the offices of these agents.

Moreover, this fecklessness and corruption of state action may extend to legislation and regulation neither focused on nor responsive to the conditions fostering the development of organized crime networks. Problems impacting the public interest may be "solved" with measures that do not comprise public service (e.g., mass surveillance unchecked by accountability), resulting in public funds supporting special interests.

However, it is not only fecklessness and corruption of state action that create conditions favorable for organized crime group development. The relationship among state, organized crime groups, and labor is complex, if not chaotic, with the social outcomes in the political economy variable with the attendant circumstances of the particular governance of the state (Koivu 2018, 62–63). Expediency of action matters. State action in prohibiting certain conduct and protecting other conduct affect the productive (e.g., market making such as narcotics and firearms distribution) and coercive (e.g., unlawful threats and violence) capacities of organized crime groups. Labor may be controlled for better or worse by organized crime groups, with the state drawing a line between unlawful labor racketeering and lawful top-down union management's corralling of rank-and-file. There is an essential give-and-take among state actors, economic elite, and racketeers such that the status quo is not existentially threatened as this would imperil the sources of income, dispositions of assets, and political influence of too many: high managerial agents, including policy makers and law-enforcers, tend first to preserve their livelihoods, placing their principals right behind them every step of the way. Thus, collusive criminal activities such as illicitly paying off labor bosses for labor peace may have favorable outcomes for these high managerial agents notwithstanding the sell-out of lower ranked individuals.

The existence and essential characteristics of (transnational) organized crime groups, whether reportedly tightly organized like the five families of New York City or loosely federated in the gig political economy of transient and expedient networked relationships, are constructed from the following realities:

1. Organized crime relationships and entities are characterized by opacity. Without transparency, there's a lack of accountability, which facilitates final and intermediate sales of good and services. One may sell and buy in secret (e.g., there's no receipt, no right of return, no formal statement of origins and supply chains). Of course, this lack of openness allows for nefarious strategies and tactics by organized crime participants (e.g., blackmail and extortion).

2. A wide range of goods and services may be offered, unhinged from the requirements and burdens of regulation and registration. The black

and gray markets are accessible well beyond that which may be sold at common retailers. One may sell and buy products and services not available elsewhere (e.g., prohibited drugs, controlled wildlife, kiddie slaves, and porn). Everything is in a sense for sale.

3. Rule of law is deprioritized. Agreements may not be enforceable in courts of law or equity; a private domain among seller, broker, and buyer is created extralegally where the goods and services are outlawed. The black and gray markets in a sense are nearer the ideal of free enterprise and pure capitalism than political economies whose warp and woof are formed under rule of law. Even the construct of competitive pricing has little relevance as the market of sellers is outside antitrust law. (However, what could be more indicative of organized crime groups operating in the upperworld than antitrust conduct? See Morrison 2020.)

However, it may be that attempts to predict the nature of organized crime groups, whether based on general evolutionary expectations of change or on a form of persistent structure such as ethnicity, are erroneous. Organized crime tends to adapt to opportunities based on attendant circumstances, implicating both traditional elements (e.g., vertical hierarchy of control) and emerging elements (e.g., horizontal cooperation among disparate groups) (Sergi and Storti 2020, 11). For better and worse, there are class, capability, competency, and skill variables at play: one cannot climb the informal hierarchy of income and decision making of organized crime solely on the basis of ethnicity. Professional skills (e.g., financial services), knowledge (e.g., criminal networks, black and gray markets), and discrete cooperative intelligence (e.g., the capability to form horizontal alliances among individuals inside and outside of core of high managerial agents) are key characteristics necessary for success.

Contrary to past paradigms, organized criminal groups do not have a distinct identity (James 2012, 226). There's no mission or vision meaningfully articulable. Organized crime groups should not be rigidly defined, and they do not have fixed attributes. Rather, organized crime is discoverable based on its activities (e.g., creation of, participation in, and facilitation of criminal markets). Moreover, they do not always exert adverse effects on society, having the demonstrated capacity to stabilize fragile and failing states (e.g., Soviet Union circa 1991). This capacity to do good should not be overstated as governance by organized criminals is not based on rules of law but grounded in providing economic opportunity in licit and illicit markets where the state fails to do so sufficiently (*Id.* at 236). Giving and obtaining favors, due presently or in the future, form the social (illicit) capital.

The natural and logical trendline of organized crime is to become legitimate, that is, to buy and sell without fear of regulators and law enforcement officials. In an ideal black universe dominated by organized crime, leadership transactions like bribery (cf. political contributions) and kickbacks (cf. finder's fees and commissions) would be socially tolerable, at least at the decision- and policy-making levels of the executive, legislative, and judicial branches of governance. The rule of law would be co-opted at the highest stage of formal hegemony by organized crime leadership and its facilitators. There would be no need for the prohibition of dishonest services as the construct and scope of honest services would be reduced in scope and effectiveness (cf. *Skilling v. United States* 2010). That is, society's standards of conduct under an organized crime-dominated regime would resemble a "might makes right" political economy, allowing such adverse outcomes as winner-takes-all.

The process and arc of organized crime do not aim for truth and justice, except where these concepts are redefined beyond recognition (cf. political contributions as speech and corporations as persons). The words would comport with official decree. The language of the rule of law as imperatives and prohibitions of conduct would be divorced from the rule of facts and evidence. Orwell would be intrigued.

Nonetheless, it may not be the state or regulating agency that is responsible for the emergence of organized crime groups. Instead, organized crime and its primary predicate of collusion erupt organically from the system of the political economy, that is, no creative and strategic genius is required to integrate disparate groups of individuals, whether formally registered as corporations or informally associated as illicit networks, in a profiteering enterprise (Jaspers 2019, 429). Thus, organized crime groups and collusive conduct (cf. antitrust offenders) are real outgrowths of the hegemonic political economy with its particular vulnerabilities. This collective illicit action is not merely an indication of a deficient inspection and oversight function administered by the state, that is, organized crime cannot be audited and investigated out of existence. Systemic vulnerability is the fertile soil for the growth of organized crime groups: collusion pays, especially in a political economy where many are desperate and vulnerable and a few have inordinate privilege and significant influence.

Organized crime is a process and output, with its actors composing an interdependent network of legitimate and illegitimate nodes or enterprises; this may be deemed the organized crime matrix, which arguably allows the most efficient and least risky method to commit crimes optimizing colluding individuals (McIllwain 2015, 34). Efficient in that many actors are ready and capable of participating in the loose but expedient structure; risk-averse in that its intransparency and decentralization limit law enforcement efforts to understand and deconstruct it.

Importantly, it is the organized crime matrix that empowers the organized crime units—whether conceived as regimes, families, syndicates, and so on. There is no boss of bosses (e.g., a role analogous to the chief executive officer or chairman of the board) in the sense conceived where the study is publicly filing corporations under the U.S. Securities and Exchange (SEC) regulations. Plans and acts get made and performed within the structure of the organized crime matrix, which persists through time and across venues. It is contingent on attendant circumstances.

Moreover, as it has been represented on multiple occasions that organized crime will sell to anyone that will pay, without scruple as to ideology, integrity, or moral principles, it fits in well with capitalist and individualist societies such as the United States (Perri and Brody 2011, 48). Thus, it is easy to conceive of organized crime as often differing little in structure and objective from commercial reporting entities (without formal compliance units and codes of ethics). The overarching objectives are to get paid and don't get caught—profitability without transparency. Imagine a structure and operations analogous to an intelligence agency dedicated to absorbing others' financial resources while peddling goods and services outside of the rule of law.

While SEC compliance is irrelevant to organized crime enterprises, a comparison of characteristics of organized crime groups and legitimate business groups proves insightful. See Table 11.1 below.

Table 11.1 Comparison of key attributes between organized crime and legitimate enterprises

Attribute	Criminal Enterprise	Legitimate Enterprise
Formation	Informal association of like-minded individuals	Formal incorporation and filing of legal documents
Means and methods	Violence, threats of violence, and fraud	Contracts and agreements
Strategy	Dominant focus on extraction of resources	Dominant focus on production/distribution
Intersection	Gambling, drugs, firearms, and loan-sharking	Gambling, drugs, firearms, and lending

Notwithstanding the differences in means and methods of conducting operations, there are many poignant similarities between organized criminal groups and legitimate business enterprises. These include:

- Dependence on access to a product line(s). A key aspect of organized crime is that it is not generally a major producer of goods. It does not manufacture pharmaceuticals (but it will facilitate the illicit purchase of opioids); it does not manufacture firearms (but it will provide the logistics to traffic illegally in firearms). For example, organized criminals extend the market to purchasers otherwise unable to access lawful markets without great difficulty (e.g., to obtain opioids lawfully, the would-be buyer must secure a script from a medical doctor and present it to a pharmacy store).
- Dependence on the capability to offer service(s). The consumer may gamble legally in state-established venues, or the consumer may gamble in illicit, unregistered mob stores. Prostitution services may be lawfully purchased in Las Vegas, NV, or prostitution services may be delivered through organized crime networks serving other venues. For example, organized criminals exploit jurisdictional differences and provide services to would-be buyers otherwise unable to travel to and from lawful venues.
- Dependence on extraction of financial resources along the supply and distribution chains. Both loan-sharking as an illicit

service and extending credit as a licit service are characterized by the extraction of financial resources from the debtor, whether as vigorish (i.e., usurious interest rates and fees) or as lawful origination fees and statutorily capped rates of interest: These accrue to the creditor without the creditor having created any goods or rendered any services to the debtor other than actions as a financial intermediary in a rentier function.

Importantly, the goals, objectives, and means and methods of persistent organized crime groups and longstanding legitimate commercial enterprises are more similar than dissimilar. The persons leading illicit racketeering and licit profit-making businesses are driven to obtain financial security as an overarching goal. This security tends to permeate the enterprises such that the skimming and earning of financial resources (e.g., cash proceeds whether obtained through extortion or right to regular salary) allows for capital (e.g., savings) accumulation. Thus, the individuals comprising these types of enterprises are engaged in a flight from actual and potential precarity. Few are secure on a long-term basis. Insecurity breeds vulnerability, which births desperation.

Objectives may be illicit (e.g., insurance fraud, bankruptcy fraud, health care fraud) or licit (e.g., manufacture, distribution, or sale of cosmetics, automobiles, or cereal), and means and methods may be unlawful (e.g., extortion, sextortion, bribery, and kickbacks) or lawful (e.g., proper preparation and submission of lowest responsible bid in a procurement program). However, these objectives and means and methods serve the goal of financial security. Organized crime groups that persist (i.e., those that are not created and dissolved *ad hoc* under a particular, limited illicit scheme) need reliable human resources and other assets (e.g., logistics support in the supply and distribution chains) as do companies publicly filing periodic reports to the U.S. Securities and Exchange Commission.

The covert rackets and the publicly filing corporation seek commercial advantages. Some may be purely illicit over the short-, medium-, and long-terms; some may be composed of individuals with firm commitments to the rule of law and ethical principles. Many are hybrid (e.g., Enron), directed, controlled, and managed under a hybrid scheme—part lawful and part unlawful, depending on the attendant circumstances.

This is not to imply that everyone is equally vulnerable to participate purposely and knowingly in criminal enterprises; however, few are immune from such temptation.

In brief, organized criminals negotiate needs not served adequately by lawful markets. Dominant market norms exclude, for example, those without creditworthiness from accessing banks and other legitimate lenders. They prevent individuals with criminal records from obtaining firearms. Market discipline, with its own routines and protocols, leaves many out. These persons, whether in times of need or greed, provide the fuel of organized crime (i.e., financial resources such as cash).

Organizing criminal activity is a complex process demanding discipline. Success depends on making the right connections with associates, obtaining adequate resources such as finance, having logistical capacity including international nodes, and many other sub-processes that need both coordination and secrecy. The general script has been written (Levi 2008, 392). The emergence into being of the organized crime group takes much planning, luck, and deficiency in state inspection, oversight, and administrative skills. Organizing crime results in the creation of extra legal markets that provide real value in the facilitation or actual provision of demanded services or goods by consumers/victims.

Indeed, it is revealing not only to analyze and discuss how organized crime develops through the language of scripts and processes but to consider why it is not more prevalent than it is, that is, how does the design and operation of society contribute to the impetus and motivation to seek profits, gains, and influence extra legally, and how does it suppress it. Markets are inherently amoral; it is the state and those materially supporting the state that aid and abet and define the attributes of the market. Specifically, the market may be legal but unfair to many. The playing field may arguably be level, but the players are differently equipped to negotiate successfully through its obstacles (e.g., barriers to financial security such as costs of housing, education, health care, and so on).

However, this is not to suggest that organized crime provides a fair exchange of value between seller and buyer. Also, it is not to suggest that the emergence of organized crime from the collaboration of individuals implies that their society and rules of law are necessarily morally or ethically deficient. The conditions that contribute to the formation of organized crime are based in freedom: decision making of individuals allows for commitment to organized crime. One can choose the extra legal pathway. Suppress freedom and the risk of organized crime arising extra legally is mitigated, though not without significant costs and externalities (e.g., an excess of state control may dampen innovation and the rate of progress).

Thus, it is important to distinguish between organized crime against the state (i.e., extra legally) and organized crime facilitated by the state (e.g., rules of law that normalize corruption).

There are no warranties or money-back guarantees in the exchange of goods and services with organized criminals; there is no recourse to courts of law or equity to enforce contracts; there is no database in the custody of the jurisdiction's secretary of state to learn of properly registered entities from which one may perform due diligence and discover the seller's character and reputation. Inherent risk is overwhelming to all but the desperate.

Moreover, a global boss of bosses is not needed. There is no routine (financial) reporting obligation. In fact, the only obligations that really matter are socially based (e.g., trust, commitment to clandestine conduct), forming the waterfall of allocation of the criminal proceeds. Common references to market-based norms mislead in the sense that the organized crime unit does not deliver its reward through dividends after accounting for profit and loss. The unit is commission-based, taking from the top, regardless of whether much remains to trickle down.

In this sense, there is a class attribute at play within organized crime. Levers of power are less contingent on ethnicity than access to opportunities within society that may be exploited. This kind of influence is rarer in the low borne than in the middle- to upper classes. Even the underworld has a socioeconomic hierarchy.

Where the take is low, the recourse is not to lawyers and accountants piecing together an accounting based on written agreements and financial reports. Instead, recourse arises from perception of breach of trust, which is a socially founded norm in the case of organized crime (e.g., the plan was to yield $X but actually returned a fraction of $X—what happened? How did the betrayal occur?) The confederation among participants in the organized crime matrix, whether closely affiliated in the same regime, more loosely affiliated in the same family, or even remotely affiliated in the case of international deals such as human, firearms, and drug trafficking, is based on similar beliefs and values. Namely, rules of law that impair the criminal objectives of the unit particularly and the matrix generally are obstacles and not the basis of commitments. Extortion and violence are permitted, even expected, among the range of responsive recourse upon breach of trust.

The organized crime matrix persists notwithstanding its essential dual natures of corrupted and corrupting because to many individuals, whether situated in the underworld as participants in organized crime or occupying positions in the upperworld as lawyers, bankers, accountants, and other facilitators of organized crime, the life of belonging to the matrix is more beneficial and secure—both from a social and financial perspective—than life in unyielding resistance to (criminal) opportunities rife within their neighborhoods, cities, and regions. The narrative of life as an organized criminal may appeal more than the narrative of the life of the dedicated servant of fast-food restaurants.

For most, it's hard to make a buck, even for professional facilitators. However, there is a definite opportunity for professionals that can disguise the monetary proceeds from criminal activities (e.g., accountants that create false entries concealing the true nature and purpose of transactions) through shell companies (e.g., created by company formation agents, including lawyers, that offer a multiplicity of accounts through which to process funds) and other attributes of the global financial system (e.g., bank secrecy regimes through which taxes may be evaded and beneficial ownership hidden) (Europol 2020, 16). Life in organized crime may be more challenging and rewarding than life as a plodding, struggling individual working for the salary that needs supplement.

The matrix may overall present superior opportunities than otherwise slaving away in the legitimate political economy. *Carpe diem* with individuals of similar attitudes, beliefs, and values may trump the struggles of negotiating through the business risks of small, medium, and large enterprises with individuals artificially forced together and superficially united in an amorphous (pseudo)meritocratic legitimate organization. Arguments presented against the corruption of abandoning the comforts of the rules-based political economy for the values-based but corrupt political economy of organized crime may just not be adequately persuasive for the so-called ordinary rank-and-file (Jacobs and Alford 2005, 15).

The organized crime matrix offers a narrative that is longstanding and powerful, displacing facts, evidence, and statistical reasoning. There is no risk calculus developed, implemented, evaluated, and tested by participants high and low in the matrix, notwithstanding evidence suggesting that commitment to the matrix is not what it appears to be. Loyalties are not ironclad but are contingent, notwithstanding shared ethnicity. Associates rat on their bosses; underbosses rat on higher bosses. Participants may be cooperating witnesses or informants and accomplices serving law enforcement agencies and not the principles and values of *omerta* or *la cosa nostra*. In material respects, the beliefs and values that hook many into the matrix are illusory, with participants ready to save themselves at the expense of other (formerly) likeminded criminals. After all, there is no retirement package or golden parachute.

Organized crime is nothing without the matrix.

> The scheme laid bare the dark underbelly of globalization. A racket concocted in far-off Malaysia came to involve people and institutions all across the world, owing to a system of elite networks seemingly fine-tuned for criminal enterprise. "Using prestigious, brand-name gatekeepers is often the key to pulling off complex financial crimes," Dennis Kelleher, CEO of the financial watchdog group Better Markets, told me. "They effectively sell their credibility and imprimatur, which criminals use to overcome their victims' skepticism. When they get caught, the enriched gatekeepers that made it all possible claim no knowledge or liability for the billions of dollars in damage done. The corruption of the enablers and their lack of accountability is what makes people so angry."
>
> —Cockburn 2020

Plausible deniability; organized crime like state intelligence agencies flees from accountability through misrepresentations and material omissions in its public discourse, if there's any at all. Organized crime is as materially misleading as any individual or collective needing to conceal its character. So long as the reputation is preserved (e.g., the richer and more exciting lifestyle of the made member), any potential character analysis (e.g., the contingency of success in organized crime is as fragile as most lawful endeavors in an overwhelmingly employment at will society like the United States and many others).

Of course, that financial and other crimes require more than a misguided and perverse individual but a depreciated and bad moral atmosphere within commerce is hardly a new thought (Evans 1859, 5). It's hard to steal big without a web of support. Rogues only get so far with only so little. To effectuate the high-valued worthwhile heist, the errant individual needs a gang of degenerates of similarly low moral character to accomplish the notoriously grand design and get off scot-free. Plunder, wash, repeat: this is the summary transaction cycle of illicit capital accumulation. Also, one may be clean-shaven and wear a suit-and-tie in his or her (mostly, him) daily affairs.

In practice, it takes a global village of cooperating professionals to facilitate big-time plunder. The matrix operates under the principle of plausible deniability, with transparency being the exception. Some jurisdictions such as the United States have opacity built into the rule of law (Zelikow, Edelman, Harrison, and Gventer 2020). Shielding disclosure of beneficial owners of corporations and empowering these legal fictions to conceal, purposely, knowingly, recklessly, or negligently the nature of transactions, including financial flows in and out of corporate entities, facilitate the successful persistence of organized crime groups. To be in organized crime is to be, by definition, not alone in the commitment to and practice of profitable criminal activity. Profit and gain generate the potential for significant corrupt influence. When profitability and capital are shrunk and absorbed at legitimate businesses, these enterprises dissolve, liquidate, or otherwise become bankrupt. Associations that do not contribute to profit and capital inside the organized crime matrix fall off, abandoned like a parka on hot summer night.

Professionals such as lawyers, bankers, accountants, and realtors contribute to the facilitation of organized crime group activities. Among other processes, these professionals enable include financial and beneficial owner secrecy and the discovery and exploitation of cross-border transactions. Conditions such as financial instability and high levels of competition (within and outside the given firm of professionals) create vulnerabilities and the willingness to accept financial crime and conduct risks that would perhaps in more auspicious and less precarious circumstances be rejected, especially in the United States where, for example, firms of attorneys may be interpreted as transient groups of individual professionals continually moving from peer-to-peer without developing loyalties and commitments to ethics and honor (Middleton and Levi 2015, 662). The professionals are part of the matrix, horizontally supporting unlawful accretions of profit, capital, and influence through organized criminal activities.

Mostly, the matrix is dedicated to service like a broker-dealer of gray and black market goods and services. It is the information and communication technology that delivers extralegally, extracting a risk premium for its assumption of potential criminal liability. It is capitalism without rules for the general welfare or public interest. Again, it is capitalism on steroids, the disposability of innumerable individuals that cannot compete successfully in a brutalized, dystopian political economy (Tudor 2019, 1251–52). A society and political economy may be assessed not so much by their high technology and comparative power of their leadership class over the rank-and-file (cf. financial services institutions, military contractors and national security firms, social media monopolies and cartels, professional managers in law and accounting) as by how or even if the attendant environment supports the ethical and moral development and redevelopment of the residents and citizens thereunder.

Of course, this is not to suggest that organized crime may thrive only under conditions of capitalism. Key here is understanding what is meant by capitalism, which as a loosely structured political economy means that private individuals rank priorities, usually leveraging their assets, income, and influence over the rule and implementation of law like the United States. The capitalist is allowed to obtain, secure, and grow his or her capital (e.g., savings) usually unrestricted by state interference or the public interest (e.g., the so-called free market).

The capability of securing special consideration and benefit of others' decision making (e.g., admittance to prestigious universities) where most others cannot occur in societies and political economies notwithstanding the macroeconomic label attached (e.g., socialist, communist, capitalist). Organized crime is a corrupted and corrupting pathway around and/or through the rule of law.

CHAPTER 12

Event-Based (i.e., the Study of Criminal Events and Collective Action as the Basis for Conclusions)

We can conceptualize organized crime as a construct dependent upon specific groups or networks, that is, there are illicit activities committed by individuals acting as a criminal enterprise (e.g., racketeering). However, it may be more fertile to theorize about organized crime as inextricably entangled with criminal markets. Groups and networks may come and go, but the illicit market persists (Albanese 2012, 2).

While the United States and Italy have focused on criminal groups (e.g., mafia, racketeer influenced and corrupt organizations), England and Wales, for example, have focused on criminal activities (Sergi 2015, 183). Neither approach may encapsulate the continuing nature of organized crime, especially at the transnational level. Undoubtedly, organized crime consists of marketing illicit goods and services that are provided collectively across diverse jurisdictions, but focusing on the group, the network, or the crime itself does not include enough information to explain how illicit markets survive dedicated decades of law enforcement activity. The supply and demand endpoints seem to generate a circuit that replicates itself notwithstanding arrests, deaths, assassinations, imprisonments, and so on. The script reiterates independently of any one will, effort, and decision making.

Thus, the conspiracy model of England and Wales and the membership model of the United States and Italy, while useful legal concepts to impose lawful punishments, are not sufficient in scope to explain organized crime (cf. Sergi 2015, 197). Moreover, even the phrasing of the term "organized crime" presumes that the activity of organizing has occurred. Organizing is not peculiar within the human species; organizing to commit unlawful acts is not unusual, currently or historically. What needs attention are the events themselves embedded in their facilitating markets; that is, the types of wrongdoing may be fundamentally crude (e.g., issuing extortionate threats) or fairly sophisticated (e.g., boiler room operations comprising securities fraud). But the events share the characteristic of unlawful exploitation of another's vulnerability to obtain profit, gain, and/or influence.

Traditionally and ironically, a distinction is made between lawful and unlawful exploitation to categorize and differentiate common white collar, socially acceptable conduct, at least in the United States (e.g., the use of sales puffery to bamboozle a customer) from prohibited organized crime conduct (e.g., the use of collusive fraud to bamboozle a client). The distinctions are nuanced, and the victim is conceivably equally impaired by both types of conduct. Thus, the study of events may make for intriguing narrative, but the study of markets yields fertile observations.

There is no organized crime without a market, and markets have the inherent potentiality of fermenting organized criminal conduct. Moreover, markets are imperfectly developed conceptions, that is, the observer cannot readily distinguish among legitimate, gray, and black markets. Moreover, markets are collusive in nature; groups of participants are needed to develop, sustain, and expand markets (e.g., custodians of funds and other assets, record keepers, exchanges, regulators in the public and private sectors, gatekeepers). There is no free market, but there are limits to state interventions over markets.

Properly, the market, and not the ethnicity of participants or other identity-based characteristics of these participants, should be the unit of analysis. The primary relevant issue is how can markets be used to further the interests of organized criminals, independently of whether the participants are wearing white collars and ties or jeans and t-shirts and independently of whether their ancestry can be traced to Palermo, Italy, or Greenwich, Connecticut. Criminal economic organizations prey on markets and exploit market participants in an unlawful network of undisclosed partnerships and informally shared incentives and financial interests.

Specifically, the criminal event is not comprised exclusively of the organized criminals' conduct. It is the conduct in the context of an enabling market that is essential to grasp. Without the facilitating market, organized crime would be a minor problem; with the aid of the market, it becomes inherently a global phenomenon, extracting resources from victims—individuals and states—and diluting the positive effects of rule of law.

Organized crime is illegitimate collective action, notwithstanding the difficulty on occasion of drawing a line between the legitimate and the illegitimate (Levin 2013, 164). For example, Enron was characterized by organized criminal economic conduct, but it was viewed as a more or less legitimate entity. Thus, organized crime in the United States involves more than a conspiracy but also participation in an illegitimate enterprise or an enterprise that acts like an illegitimate enterprise, excluding hybrid organizations like Enron, WorldCom, Wells Fargo, and so on that act in part like criminal conspiracies intentionally creating unlawful conduct and in part like legitimate enterprise, properly filing financial reports and tax returns. Of course, the hybrid organization is the more harmful yet ambiguous collective as it is viewed as something it is not, viz., legitimate.

The essentially banal and common property denoted "collective action" is deceptive in its power to direct, control, or influence. Small groups of individuals acting in concert can wreak great harms (or accomplish wonderful goals and objectives). The peculiarity of organized crime groups is their inherent exclusion from propriety by the state; that is, collective action toward criminal objectives is not recognized as a legitimate group activity. There is no corporate limited liability from the law sourced in participation in organized crime groups; there are favorable schemes of tax administration resulting from obtaining funds flowing from their illicit activities. The collective of organizing criminals is not protected, unless it mimics successfully the legitimate organization. Thus, since directing financial flows to and from tax havens is consistent with tax avoidance strategies of legitimate business, the adoption of these practices and procedures by illicit collectives hiding underneath a shell or front company should be wholly expected.

The market creates opportunity for licit and illicit collectives. However, since the illicit organization cannot commit to transparency and accountability in reporting to regulators and the public at large, such an organization lacks rigorous and invariable definition. It is continually in flux, operating and presenting itself with as much legitimacy as practicable. Moreover, without robust mandatory disclosure schemes adopted by jurisdictions domestically and internationally, the opacity of beneficial owners that compose the cadre of high managerial agents of illicit collectives remains a vague shadow without real identity of the straw men. The rule of law does not permit accurate and complete attribution of the profits, gains, and assets in the accounts, which are protected by jurisdictions racing to the bottom for a small fee, to the cadre of high managerial agents and influential professional facilitators.

A focus on the errant collective would lead the criminal investigator on a worldwide pathway of obfuscation and legal niceties. Activity profitable for the lawyer but not so much conducive to truth of ownership, management, and control of the collective. There's got to be a better way to know the network and vectors commonly referred to as transnational organized crime by criminal investigators.

CHAPTER 13

Epistemology and Sources of Knowledge

Organized crime is to a significant extent whatever the law-makers declare; its scale is measured by what the criminal investigators and public prosecutors pursue. However, while the rule of law determines that which is categorized an organized criminal activity or an organized crime group, the law is not the only relevant factor. There must be predicate or on-the-ground conduct (i.e., evidence of facts of operation in the case of criminal activities and persistence in time in the case of organized crime groups or enterprises). Not any coalescing of individuals or the plans of any rogue individual mature into organized crime groups and acts. Crucial information about how to succeed must exist and be shared among key individuals (e.g., how to avoid detection of the logistics of the criminal pathway, how to create safe physical venues within which to plan and regroup, how to secure advance warning of the law enforcement authorities' counter-actions and strategies to arrest the crime and its actors) (Dittmar 2020). This information is essential to dominate a region, if not merely to become effective in the criminal operation.

Thus, the distinction between covert and overt criminal conduct needs reflection. A period of time after planning and eliciting cooperation among key actors must elapse before overtly exercising criminal operations. This below the tip-of-the-iceberg underworld activity may ultimately determine which organized criminal groups become notorious and effective and which fail to get off the ground or experience its members getting arrested prematurely (at least from the perspective of the criminal actors). To a significant extent, taking resources from the upperworld and redefining the character of these criminal proceeds is the transactional circuit.

Criminal activities may be raised in profile as comprising threats to the public weal and national security. Not all of these elevations in profile and threat assessments are valid and reliable (Lavorgna and Sergi 2016, 182). As public funds and society's attention are taken and pushed from one existential threat to another (e.g., formerly, the five mafia crime families based in New York City; presently, transnational cybercrimes emanating from loosely affiliated individuals in dispersed geographies), the opportunity for fame and fortune exists for aggressive and self-promoting public prosecutors and criminal investigators—with the fame owing to the power of one's public position and the fortune following dividend like in the private sector.

In brief and truth, little is known about organized crime groups apart from what authorities and scholars declare. The public at large can hardly correct for systematic biases influencing the work product. Peer review may cling too tightly to what was denoted brilliant years, if not decades, before, without the exercise of critical thinking applied to the current state of reliable evidence. The epistemology of organized crime and its groupings, local, regional, and transnational, is fraught with quantitative and qualitative errors and biases in reasoning. Studies are ordinarily not replicable, having been created under specific and limited geographic conditions of the past. Frankly, work products that articulate properly the limitations of what passes for knowledge would not likely result in promotions at law enforcement agencies or tenure in higher education. Humility has little influence there, and the modest succumb to the immodest, with truth a casualty of groupthink and tenure-track.

Information risk is inherently high. Predictive objective probabilities are compromised by special circumstances attendant to the variety of geographies, occupations, and commitments and integrity of law enforcement officials. For example, in a kakistocracy, not only would the rules of law not be applied to politically influential persons (cf. crony capitalism) but the rules of law themselves would be redefined to make the corrupt lawful (e.g., campaign contributions without *quid pro quos* that are not deemed bribes, and independent expenditures not formally coordinated by political campaigns that are not deemed corruptive) (National Conference of State Legislatures 2017). Conduct formerly prosecuted in the United States as honest services fraud was reduced in scope to apply only to schemes of kickbacks and bribes in violation of a fiduciary duty because honesty in fact was deemed unconstitutionally vague

(Foster 2019, 2). That the highest court in the country could not define honesty may, assuming the risk of oversimplification, sum up the problem as no other brief statement can.

> "When I use a word," Humpty Dumpty said, in rather a scornful tone, "it means just what I choose it to mean—neither more nor less." "The question is," said Alice, "whether you can make words mean so many different things." "The question is," said Humpty Dumpty, "which is to be master—that's all."
>
> —(Carroll 1872)

Corporations are persons; money represents speech; independent expenditures indirectly favoring a political candidate are due influence. Knowing about organized crime groups, including economic and transnational groupings, requires seeing the ordinary and comprehensible in the extraordinary and opaque: there is nothing done within the range of activities of organized crime groups that does not have its roots in common commercial transactions. Odd actions (e.g., the so-called pledge of *omerta*) are tangential conduct. That which comprises the essential substance of organized crime groups may be analogously found in social and country clubs worldwide; that which creates bonds among participants in an organized crime group is similar to that which holds together a police squad or prosecutors' unit: we are greater than any one of us; to accomplish our objectives is to empower each of us. There's a certain level of "rules be damned" potentiality in nearly everyone.

The political economy is influenced by its leadership class, which may direct with disproportionate power the formation and interpretation of the rule of law. Moreover, that which is known about organized crime groups, corruption, fraud, dishonesty, and official acts is to a significant extent that which has obtained a high priority within public policy discussions as determined by the leadership class without sufficient countervailing power to rebut or modify the controlling narrative. This, of course, is not to justify criminal activities such as murder and extortion, organized or not; it also is not intended as a valid excuse to ignore official corruption or wrongfully elevate threats beyond the actual gravity and frequency of social harms posed by the threat.

In practice, it may be the corrupting of public officials by organized criminals that may contribute most to a global and burgeoning criminal enterprise (Johnson 2020b). This may not be a popular narrative to discuss in the corridors of power within the legitimate political economy. How products, including investment vehicles, and how services, including gambling, offered through legitimate pathways, locally and lawfully, may blend without clear demarcation and identifiers into the illegitimate globalized network comprised of parasitical individuals. Politicians, bureaucrats, commercial entities, including financial institutions and professional service providers, are among the types of actors within the globally linked criminalized networks that extract financial resources along the supply chain. The key term is "networks" as plurality and multiplicity characterize the web. This is worse than complex; it is chaotic.

In theory, what is known with high levels of certainty (forever subject to adjustment) is that which survives rigorous, scientific, and peer-reviewed testing. In practice, what is known is that which is released as official crime statistics. If it's not measured, it may not exist officially. The government has a monopoly on public prosecution and criminal investigation, with its results occasionally challenged in courts of law (assuming adequacy of financial resources on the part of the defendant) but mostly subjected to plea bargaining through deep-pocketed public prosecutors supported by institutions.

Moreover, scholarly approaches will invoke the expertises of psychology, sociology, and criminology, if not others also, to explain the origins, development, persistence, and redevelopment of organized crime groups. Undoubtedly, each of these expertises is helpful in its own way. However, the designation of organized criminal enterprise or gang is the result of actions and decisions of those entrusted with the design and implementation of the rule of law. There is certainly nothing sinful or morally suspect about organizing, and there is no shame in striving to obtain financial resources and a measurable influence in the affairs of the political economy. It is how these dedicated actions are defined and interpreted by society that create the appellation of organized crime group.

Frankly, the public at large abides without a sense of proportionality as the discourse is dominated officially. While one is free to discard or challenge the prevailing ideology, one is not at liberty to avoid the costs (e.g., status, publication history) from excluding oneself from the reference narratives composing the status quo.

Not only are the processes inherent in contemplating and furthering illicit objectives through unlawful means relevant to knowing about organized crime, but the processes determining what is prohibited (e.g., once, booze in the United States) and what is not (e.g., political campaign contributions and lobbying in the United States) are also material to ascertain context and proportion. Generally, what we know about organized crime groups is what we are told about organized crime groups through education, training, and interpretation of formal (usually, law enforcement) experience. One seeks and obtains the prevailing general consensus about organized crime groups through these mechanisms. One's knowledge is overwhelmingly indirect, that is, organized crime groups are not empirically observable like the apparent rising of the sun in the morning. It is pieced together in reliance on self-serving cooperative witnesses, deal-seeking informants, public disseminations of criminal trials, and lofty and alarming pronouncements of the organs of the media and government, including legislators, executives, and judges, among other sources, who may be motivated largely by the prospect of increases to their budgets.

Both the validity and reliability of the evidence and data used to create and publish the theories and concepts implicated in ordinary discussions, Hollywood entertainment (e.g., *The Sopranos, Goodfellas, The Godfather*), and law-makers' punishment regimes (e.g., the Racketeer Influenced and Corrupt Organizations Act, Title 18 U.S. Code Chapter 96) need reexamination. The effects from puffery, mythology, and rumor infect these discussions and analyses with unquantifiable but likely material error. The biases are systematic. Whether the reference narratives fill in the gaps resulting from primarily indirect knowledge or wildly supplement this domain of knowledge with unreal specters of evil geniuses and well-oiled nefarious organizational regimes is hard to discern, sometimes.

For example, the use of leniency programs (e.g., formal inducements such as lessening of punishment granted to accomplices that testify against other organized crime members) has been suggested to exert positive effects on prosecution and deterrence of organized crime figures in Italy (Acconcia, Immordino, Piccolo, and Rey 2014,

1137–40). Understandably, the positive effect on prosecutions would be an expected result from the introduction of accomplice and witness testimonies; however, the idea that the narrative becomes more valid and reliable from extension of prosecutorial favor does not seem clearly persuasive any more than the use of bribes and kickbacks assures the selection of the most responsible lowest bidder on a public procurement contract. The bias introduced by incentive systems, especially leniency programs under which prolonged periods of incarceration are at stake, is not readily overcome.

Of course, none of this is to aver that the five families in New York City did not exist and thrive for decades; indeed, they had international personal and professional associations to facilitate organized criminal activities, especially in Italy. However, what seems underemphasized is that these were five purportedly distinct criminal operations led by different bosses centered in one metropolitan area. Even in such a limited geography, there was space for many to make extralegally outsized profits and gains and exert significant influence in the legal political economy. Customer allocation (cf. antitrust law) in an expanding local economy was as much responsible for the persistence of these informally disparate criminal groups as any top-down influence of the big man syndrome. This is important because organized crime persists where the conditions are right and the men are willing—much more so than persistence due to the powers of great but evil men.

The five organized crime groups comprised a cartel that co-existed for much of the period—a fact suggesting that even illicit power in the heyday of the New York City mob era could be shared among several, casting doubt on the idea that any one of these families, bosses, underbosses, and corrupt associations in the political economy had the hegemonic capacities inherent in inflated accounts of five-family mafia infiltration and influence. These inflated accounts were substantially developed, supported, and disseminated widely through mass media, trade journals, and scholarly publications largely due to the direct and indirect efforts of public prosecutors prone to self-promotion, advancement and diversification of professional career(s), and plain unreflective errors in reasoning (e.g., lack of proportionality in analysis and synthesis of underlying data).

Moreover, the hyperbolic accounts of the dominant opinion-makers fed into other works of art such as film and television. Law and order was (and likely is) the overarching goal for the proper state of society—a state ostensibly and existentially threatened by larger than life figures created not only by racketeering investigators, public prosecutors, and federal legislators, but by commercial studios propagandizing and selling the boss and crew as viable threat to the peaceful state. Tougher laws brought more power, including the bully pulpit to play the man in the white hat— veritable savior of society from the ever encroaching yet covert and sinister influence of the (predominantly) men in black hats. One does not achieve social and elite status by crushing a bug, however, giant killing may do the trick.

The incentives of the sources of data and evidence (e.g., informants seeking sweetheart deals with the government), as well as the incentives of the racketeering investigators and film studios, compound the potential bias and error. Facts on the ground may be clear (e.g., a dead body washing up from the East River in New York City), but the background and context woven therefrom is invariably sewn and dyed to suit the storyteller. Importantly, what we think we know is not only derived from sources outside of our personal knowledge (i.e., assuming we are not global gangsters) but contingent upon the competency and integrity of experts with clear and underweighted personal and professional agendas leveraging an inadequacy of reliable data and evidence.

Some researchers have advised that multiple triangulations with respect to research may substitute as an alternative for data and evidence validity and reliability obtained from scientific methodologies such as regression analyses founded on competent and sufficient data. Thus, knowledge is the result of sifting through a multiplicity of theories, observations, sources of data, and methodologies (Arsovska 2008, 46). Of course, such an approach is vulnerable to biases in subjectivity notwithstanding snowballing across a diversity of expert panels: as reasonable individuals may differ in their conclusions and so may experts, especially in the social sciences where replication of studies may be fairly criticized. Sometimes, data and evidence do not drive public policy, but public policy and preferences of influential persons (e.g., economic elite, organized trade groups) may corral the production and distribution of generally accepted theories and official positions, hardening these into a false consciousness of knowledge where it really represents only expertized belief—policy directing and controlling the data.

To date, knowledge (cf. myth, false belief) about organized crime is primarily ideologically based and maintained almost exclusively by law enforcement efforts and findings. Discussion and analysis about root causes and empirical evidence of the true risk factors contributing to its development are scarce. The approach itself may be questioned: instead of accepting without sufficient competent evidence panel opinions drawn from expert law enforcement officials, the researchers should refocus with a risk assessment perspective that incorporates private and public sector opportunities appealing to organized crime strengths and networks (Albanese 2009, 417). Ideology suppresses the discovery of knowledge of causes and effects that would empower analysts to answer the basic question—how do we know about organized crime? Perhaps, too much is omitted, and too much is falsely explained.

A focus on risks presented by the market and public institutions would demonstrate the banality of organized crime in many respects. It is a composite of rent extraction in high profitability opportunity structures (e.g., loan-sharking), a commission merchant in black markets (e.g., narcotics, human trafficking), and an enterprise able and willing, where necessary or desirable, to engage in violent activities, including making extortionate threats. Research directed with this focus would leave behind obsolete theories of organized crime as the other and reveal its commonality (but for the violence) with much of what transpires as legitimate small-to-medium-sized businesses.

Indeed, a strong argument may be developed suggesting strongly that organized crime seeks its own destruction through morphing into legitimate commerce (e.g., bootleggers in the prohibition era of the United States), Organized crime is less a way of life than a means of survival for many and thriving for a few. It is contingent of profitability, gain, and influence structures in the political economy. To know organized crime is to know how much legitimate commerce shares its attributes.

Knowledge about organized crime risk is comprised of empirical data about the structure and operations of groups of individuals, whether tightly or loosely associated, committing serious criminal offenses. Generally, undercover policing (including the use of cooperating witnesses and informants) and electronic surveillance (e.g., wiretaps, bugs) are the key law enforcement variables deployed to produce knowledge about organized crime (Jacobs and Gouldin 1999, 54).

Therefore, the public sector, including public prosecutors, law enforcement agencies, and independent regulatory agencies, is the primary source for such knowledge. Implicitly, this process of creating knowledge is influenced by careerism of public servants (e.g., building resumes); explicitly, this process is also shaped by factors outside of this source such as an independent and well-motivated media, pressures from non governmental organizations and civil society organizations, the civil law bar through its own private litigation (e.g., Racketeer Influenced and Corrupt Organizations civil actions originating in the United States), and grassroots' expressions of policy preferences.

Thus, organized crime risk is created dynamically and subject to adjustment as conditions in the political economy change, including the reordering of priorities (cf. diversion of law enforcement and intelligence agencies' resources to counter terrorism risk after 9/11 in the United States). Importantly, information about organized crime is subject to its own temporal and political biases and risks.

The public sector contributes to knowledge about organized crime (e.g., through effective and true criminal investigations and public prosecutions) and to false mythologies about organized crime (i.e., exaggerations about criminal groups' structure and activities to buttress professional and political careers). Additionally, the public sector may be a part of organized crime (Rowe, Akman, Smith, and Tomison 2013, 5). Collectively, this information risk demands calibration of both official and popular conceptions and theories about organized crime's scope and influence and actual conduct.

The public sector is the organ and source of the extant knowledge and mythology about organized crime groups. Through public sector action, the threat of organized crime is communicated and assessed, however inaccurately.

Additionally, analysts and scholars are found in non governmental and private sector nonprofit entities and institutions, which perform many legitimate roles in society, including the education of the public at large about crime and society. Key for-profit private sector entities and institutions include mass and specialized media. Of course, the attorneys' bars such as the American Bar Association and state and local bar associations also provide education about crime and misconduct risks.

All of these institutions collectively provide a useful service to the public at large, though the availability of competing, if not deflating, reference narratives is not common. That is, the uninformed audience hears "one side of the story." Moreover, the predominant narrative results in publication bias with authors that pretty much follow the status quo position more likely to have their voices recognized.

CHAPTER 14

Operations and Functioning of Organized Crime Groups

At their core, legitimate enterprises and organized crime and racketeering enterprises seek to exchange their goods and services for financial resources, especially electronic cash (e.g., bank deposits). Alternatively, other financial resources may be received such as bulk cash or cryptocurrency, which may comprise an intermediate source of wealth before realization as electronic cash in a financial institution. Resources such as bulk cash and cryptocurrency are not immediately useful to liquidate certain obligations, including tax liabilities, limiting their ultimate exchange value. Few assets are more liquid than a checking account with JP Morgan Chase.

As an artificial illegal construct, there is no formal purpose to organized crime groups separate and apart from the pursuits of profitability, gains, and influence. In this sense, they are in the same family as legal fictions colloquially known as corporations. These entities function in ways that enhance their capacities of profitability and persistence. Usually, they don't exist for the single big score, then dissolve. More often, they provide an alternative pathway to obtain financial (e.g., cash in the bank) and economic (e.g., real estate) resources, as well as to further ideological objectives (e.g., terrorism's goal of subverting a given political regime).

Organized crime groups are real (i.e., informal associations in fact) like legitimate incorporated commercial enterprises (i.e., formal associations by operation of law). They have leadership, and they have coordination among disparate parts. They work toward absorbing others' financial resources, obtaining others' products and services, coercing others' decision making, and so on. Organized crime groups exist to facilitate wrongdoing as defined by a given political regime (e.g., the U.S. statutory criminal laws). Often, their conduct is criminal (e.g., extortion) and/or tortious (e.g., unlawful interference with contractual relations). While they may form agreements with associates, competitors, and victims, they do not rely so much on formal contracts (notwithstanding mainstream and colloquial use of the term contract killing). Credible threats of extortion work way faster.

Organized crime traverses local, state, and national boundaries. It is a global phenomenon, using land, air, and sea as the physical pathways to profit, that is, the pathways are lawful, but the method may be unlawful. However, profitability is not the only concern: the U.S. national security issues are raised by the capacity of organized terrorist organizations such as the Taliban and Hezbollah to cross borders to obtain and launder financial funds through illicit means (e.g., drug trafficking, insider trading) (Lawfare (blog) 2019).

In brief, the operations of organized crime groups may be identified by the presence of one or more of the following types of objectives:

- To obtain cash (bulk and electronic, with the latter greatly exceeding in value the former)
- To obtain illicit goods and services and support black and gray markets (e.g., counterfeit goods, opioids)
- To distribute illicit goods and services (e.g., arms, support of terrorism)
- To invest in legitimate enterprises and clean illicit financial flows

The transactions supporting the accomplishment of these objectives are neither recorded accurately and completely in books and records nor examined independently and routinely by public auditors. Moreover, even the exhaustive and intrusive efforts of criminal investigators rarely result in any report resembling a fair and true accounting of transactional history of the enterprise. While the pursuit of objectives noted above would exclude legitimate commercial pursuits, overlap in operations and functionality between the organized crime group and the legitimate enterprise may be found in the examination of financial flows, with the former's illicit and the latter's licit.

Organized crime groups ultimately rely on the financial services industry to make financial resources available to their broad membership in the desired currency (usually, U.S. dollar accounts in a financial institution).

Money laundering is essentially concealing the taint of illicitly obtained funds (i.e., financial resources). It is a process resulting in the obscuring of the audit trail such that evidence disclosing the actual nature of the originating transactions (e.g., drug purchases, firearms sales) is not transparent. Briefly, money laundering is the intersecting criminal activity shared by legitimate actors behaving badly such as politicians hiding ill-gotten public funds and illegitimate actors pursuing unlawful objectives exclusively such as fully committed organized criminals. Whether the processes are acquiring public/private assets and financial resources, controlling/dampening law enforcement agency and regulator supervisory efforts, or capturing/influencing banks and similar financial institutions, the conduct of both organized criminals and corrupt politicians demonstrate shared values and use of common means and methods (United Nations Office on Drugs and Crime 2019).

Thus, the functioning of organized crime groups is similar to legitimate enterprises with respect to protection of financial resources. Whereas the legitimate enterprise has far greater tolerance of transparency within the rule of law, the illicit enterprise functions to further the goals of self-preservation and participant prosperity through tax secrecy and tax haven asset protection jurisdictions. Unsurprisingly, these jurisdictions also protect the so-called legitimate enterprises (e.g., the bank secrecy laws of former British Commonwealth colonies and dependencies protect licit as well as illicit transactional proceeds).

The sharing of functionality and goals between such apparently disparate enterprises may be expected and explained as legitimate enterprises face an almost irresistible urge to conform to criminogenic pressures (Glebovskiy 2019, 443). Profits extracted from gray and black market participation may be significant. The overlap of functionality may be deemed somewhat unavoidable in far too many cases because so many of the tactics used by organized crime groups are successful (e.g., criminal proceeds are hidden, disguised, and later used without detection through opaque and misdirecting shell companies in secrecy jurisdiction).

Intransparency benefits the legitimate as well as the illegitimate. Where resources are scarce, competitive pressures are great, and winner-take-all rules dominate, the functioning of the organized crime group resembles too much the functioning of the legitimate/quasi-legitimate enterprise (e.g., Enron).

International Tax Havens and Tax Secrecy Jurisdictions

Transnational organized crime like most crime is driven by the profit, gain, and influence motives. The opacity of international finance aids and abets the successful commission of transactional organized crime (World Customs Organization 2019). Layers upon layers of legal fictions (e.g., shell companies) located in multiple jurisdictions (e.g., Cyprus, Cayman Islands) formed and sustained by fee-seeking facilitators (e.g., lawyers, accountants, company formation agents) combine to create a nearly impenetrable (dark) web linking together illicit activities and corrupt individuals. In brief, it's hard to know what's going on in these closely held, far-flung corporate entities. Participants doing bad things tend not to flag their misconduct.

These shell companies are used to receive and distribute proceeds of illicit activities. Funds flow from the provision of illegal goods (e.g., drugs, firearms, counterfeit/gray market consumer items) and services (e.g., loan-sharking, human trafficking, bribery, and kickback schemes) to be laundered through the shell companies of tax haven and tax secrecy jurisdictions—the opacity allows the safe flow of large monetary sums, whether aggregated from frequent or big ticket transactions into and out of the shell. Within the shell, the financial resources are protected against incurious local governments and unknowing foreign governments. In a sense, some are paid not to see.

Moreover, with the advent and commercial viability of financial technology (fintech) electronic transfers are the norm, domestically and internationally. These are characterized by high amounts of debits and credits moving funds from place-to-place and depositary-to-depositary under a labyrinthine scheme of difficult to follow and difficult to attribute to any natural person organizing principles. The convoluted structure is by design and not a bug. The financial flows are much faster than the applied intelligence of criminal investigators can anticipate or even monitor, even with mutual legal assistance treaties.

Patently legitimate enterprises can hold and conceal cash and capital accounts of great magnitude. For example, reinsurance companies and other financial services providers such as hedge funds may accumulate financial resources without serious question and forensic examination. These financial service providers are often key businesses in tax havens and tax secrecy jurisdiction, providing license fees and other transfers of financial resources to otherwise revenue-starved governments and creating a veritable race to the bottom. Integrity may not pay for essential government services as well as reckless, amoral, and unethical regulatory oversight pays. Integrity is more expensive in the short- and medium terms than looking the other way. Perhaps the thinking goes—better to receive recurring streams of income from licensing fees and modest levels of taxes than to prohibit, detect, then fine. The jurisdiction may prefer a secure annual annuity than a lump sum; probity and punishment exacted against one financial institution may deter many others from on-shoring.

Of course, what's going on in the offshore tax havens and secrecy jurisdictions is not limited to venues and islands difficult to locate on a map. The superstructure supporting organized crime and their extended associations in fact operate domestically in local banks, also. Deposits of criminal proceeds become routine. Secrecy is paramount by operation of law in many states of the United States (e.g., Delaware, Nevada). Financial flows across and into U.S. dollar accounts at money center banks (e.g., JP Morgan Chase, Citibank) are also routine. A superstructure that places financial and legal confidentiality and privacy objectives higher than a commitment to understand the substance of monetary transactions implicitly promotes unaccountable conduct, including organized crime activities, by undisclosed actors.

How organized crime groups accomplish their objectives is as much an issue centering on strategies as it is on tactics. The relationship between the government and these illicit private sector parties varies across jurisdictions, with opportunities distributed unevenly transnationally. Organized crime in the United States is similar to and different from organized crime in Japan: jurisdiction and attendant circumstances matter, offering disparate opportunity structures that transform in time.

Organized crime in New York City in the 1960s is not equivalent in all material respects to organized crime in New York City in the 21st century.

Often, legitimate businesses and organized crime groups are contrasted and compared. Whatever their similarities, organized crime groups are not averse to using violent means to accomplish their goals, whereas such a tactic by a legitimate business would attract the attention of police and comprise an undesirable means and method to obtain profit and gain (Croall 2010, 342). Legitimate business cannot saliently commit extortion. Clandestine organized crime groups, where responsibility and command-and-control are distributed without demonstrable attribution to a formal hierarchy of chain of command, do commit extortionate and violent acts evident in streets and households worldwide.

However, organized criminal activities, whether exposed and mediated by the mechanisms of the rule of law (e.g., the criminal investigator and public prosecutor) or undetected by these mechanisms and falsely assumed non existent, are mediated through means and methods designed to accomplish criminal objectives. Generally, the organized crime group engages in the following actions:

1. Conduct, including plans, designed to facilitate illicit ends such as the sale of drugs and firearms proscribed by law. This set of conduct is well known by the public through depictions of fact and promotion of myth in mass media and specialized scholarship.
2. Conduct, including plans, composed of illicit means such as the bribery of public officials to effectuate corrupt private and public decision- and policy making. This set of conduct is less understood as absence or rarity of evidence is wrongfully inferred by the public (and disseminated by mass media and specialized scholarship) as evidence of absence, that is, a false negative.

The overarching goal is secrecy. The objectives are criminal, and the means and methods are unlawful.

Where rule of law is less aggressively applied with respect to some transfers of financial resources (e.g., political campaign contributions and independent expenditures in support of public policies in the United

States) than others (e.g., payments to child pornographers), the implementation of rule of law creates its own domains of priorities, knowledge, and ignorance. What is publicly known about the drug cartels in Mexico dwarfs what is publicly known about deal-making in the U.S. Congress, where the knowledge seeker merely focuses on traditional indicia of organized crime influence such as criminal convictions. Thus, the success of organized crime groups depends on minimizing and (re)directing that which gets investigated and prosecuted.

This is not to suggest that official statistics about organized crime are invariably useless, but they omit and exclude many actual predicate acts that would comprise organized criminal conduct if investigated and prosecuted (cf. false negatives). The rates of error and bias are not empirically and impartially quantifiable through commonly accepted measures of validity and reliability. Adopting the presumption that these errors and biases even out over the long-term (i.e., they are random) is not satisfactory. In fact, the assumptions of randomness and full and fair disclosure of reliable estimates of (transnational) organized economic crime by official sources are problematic, given the opportunity structures at work (e.g., pay to play barriers to entry).

The effectiveness of methods is not an issue that may be firmly fixed as a set of tactics or playbook the same across jurisdictions and temporal intervals. Things change gradually or otherwise—attendant circumstances give rise to the methodology or ways in which criminal means and objectives are realized in practice, leading to the following useful categories to be considered in the discussion of means to ends:

- Methods reputedly under sovereignty-supported organized crime (e.g., does the government implicitly support organized economic crime through its failure to control or punish such activity?)
- Methods reputedly independent of sovereignty support (e.g., does the government demonstrate a willingness and capacity to limit and sanction organized economic crime?)
- Methods focused on specific criminal acts (e.g., are acts comprising extortion, gambling, prostitution, drugs,

human trafficking, firearms trafficking fully investigated and
prosecuted from origin to beneficiary?)

Organized criminals don't seek to maximize their utility from wrongful conduct; they seek to commit actions that are unlikely to be detected
and punished seriously. The subjective willingness and capacity to act
extralegally depends on the relevant governments' enforcement of law
and regulation.

While it might have been simpler in the past to confine organized
crime to notorious crime families, the extent of criminal activities
requiring the participation of actors located across the globe should not
be underestimated. The value of counterfeit goods seizures, including
footwear, wallets, electronics equipment, apparel, and jewelry, at the
U.S. borders was estimated at $1.4 billion during the fiscal year 2018
(U.S. Immigration and Customs Enforcement 2019). The supply chain is
structured, often apparently legitimate but actually illicit, and hard to isolate (beyond a reasonable doubt) (U.S. Attorney's Office Central District
of California 2019). These illegal activities implicate domestic and international fraud and other crimes to be conceived as a dynamic, non stationary
web of interlocking and interacting processes thwarting transparency and
accountability by design.

CHAPTER 15

Transformation of Organized Crime Groups in Theory and Practice

Enterprises change—adapt or perish. Formerly, the low-tech environment of society generally enabled organized criminals to use low-tech methods successfully. For example, the use or threatened use of violence makes extortion; this may be accomplished without high-tech. However, add high-tech and extortion is possible long distance, including the hijacking of websites, sextortion, and discovery of the vulnerable many miles away. The computer has become more valuable than the car or even the firearm to effectuate organized crime.

However, not everything has changed. Secrecy and intransparency are still essential: organized crime is not overtly capitalized through Nasdaq or the New York Stock Exchange (NYSE). Its capital increases surreptitiously in accounts undisclosed or under-disclosed. Moreover, organized crime does not issue financial statements, neither audited nor reviewed, through the U.S. Securities and Exchange Commission. It is not a club that can be joined directly through the worldwide web, yet it comprises an intangible web among participants, facilitators, and beneficiaries for communication of instruction and secretion of assets.

The closest socially accepted analogue would be intelligence agencies such as the U.S. Central Intelligence Agency (CIA) that operate largely without adequate direct inspection and oversight by the public. Intransparency enables wrongdoing by preventing exposure; that of which we are unaware proceeds at its own unchecked pace. Moreover, there is no inspector general with immediate oversight responsibility for organized crime.

As organizations become too large and unwieldy, they collapse or significantly shrink (e.g., the traditional five mafia families in the

New York City metropolitan area). However, some small, effective groups become larger (e.g., smaller Mexican groups morphing into larger cartels) (Clancy 2019). However, the center cannot hold and distributed activity is the norm.

Then as now organized crime is dependent on profitability (i.e., the accumulation of surplus financial resources) (Mob Museum n.d.). Profitability is the residual interest after revenues have been extorted (e.g., protection money, sextortion demands); after funds have been received from sales of illicit goods (e.g., drugs, firearms), and obtained from other means (e.g., gambling, stock swindles). Expenses paid to associates and other facilitators (e.g., lawyers, corrupted government officials) signal a cost of doing business. In brief, financial resources are boosted from the marks (e.g., customers—willing and not willing) and repercussions, potential or actual, are fixed (i.e., conflicts deescalated or deflated, if discovered at all) through influential connections with criminal investigative agencies, public prosecutors, the judiciary, the civil bar, and so on. Indeed, organized crime effectiveness depends not only on internal resources but external factors.

Traditionally, organized crime groups such as the New York City-based five crime families of the Gambinos, Luccheses, Bonannos, Colombos, and Genoveses could survive and thrive by their own wit, connections, and intimidation. These attributes are still important, but the top-down organizational structure was too vulnerable to withstand the new law enforcement tools and policy changes extended to the U.S. Department of Justice. Moreover, this top-down organizational approach to crime management was overstated in efficacy as the required influence spread from primarily local venues to a globalized village of participants and facilitators. Merely being able to corrupt the local police force was not enough.

In modernity, the gig organized crime matrices exploit opportunity structures that demand flexibility in reach by organized criminals. Presently, the flatter supply and value chains lack rigorous centralization, with decentralization essential for thriving illicitly; this distributed web-like superstructure is intangible, not subject to extirpation by law enforcement agencies based exclusively on Long Island, New York or primarily in Washington, D.C. The problem is cross-border—transnational.

Compared to earlier models of organized crime such as top-down hierarchical organizational structures, organized crime has become transformed along with the macro trend of globalization of national political economies, the result of which is an international and fluid network of criminal actors and facilitators more often than not adept in the tools of modernity (e.g., computer-based methods of committing and concealing crime) (Bjelopera and Finklea 2012a, 2). Presently, organized crime at the local, regional, and global levels is modeled on licit and illicit network development and sustainability.

> In short, networks constitute the basic social form that permits inter-organizational interactions of exchange, concerted action and joint production.
>
> —(Bruns 2015, 166)

In lieu of a predominantly vertical and pyramidal structure, a horizontal, cross-border, virtual highway with informal toll booths serving as nodes from which and to which communications about logistics and financial flows travel.

Perhaps, the most mysterious attribute of organized crime groups is their initial capitalization. Analysts can trace financial flows and discover exchanges of real goods and services provided for cash, but where did the capital come from? Query if the five families were stripped of resources and high managerial agents, what entities provided the necessary substitution, and how so? Have organized crime core activities such as drugs, firearms, human trafficking, sex slaves, child pornography, gambling, prostitution, and so on been largely eradicated? Statistically, Figure 15.1 graphically indirectly suggests that law enforcement's assault on the five families in the 1980s had little effect on subsequent narcotics and drugs prosecutions by the U.S. Department of Justice.

Also, observe the trend of federally prosecuted weapons offenses in Figure 15.2 below. The statistics suggest indirectly but strongly that the take down of the five families had little positive effect on the persistence and growth of weapons offenses.

Moreover, the trend of federal organized crime prosecutions, peaking in the Clinton administration, suggests that organized crime, as least

Federal Judicial: U.S.
Narcotics/Drugs
prosecuted

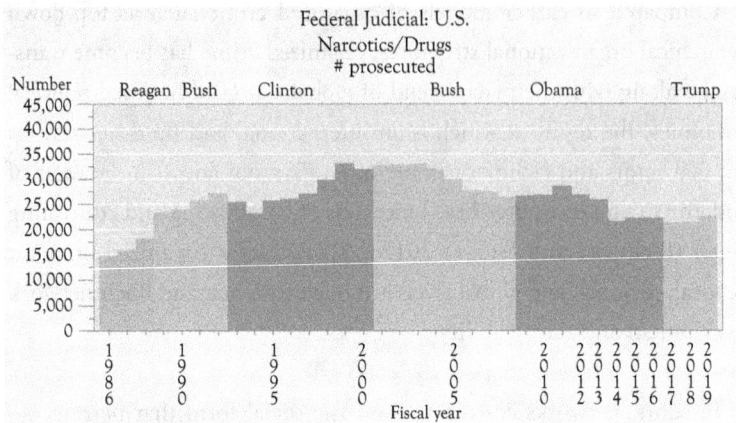

Figure 15.1 Federal narcotic and drug prosecutions, fiscal years 1986–2019

Source: Transactional Records Access Clearinghouse at Syracuse University (TRACfed)

Federal Judicial Direct: U.S.
Weapons
prosecuted

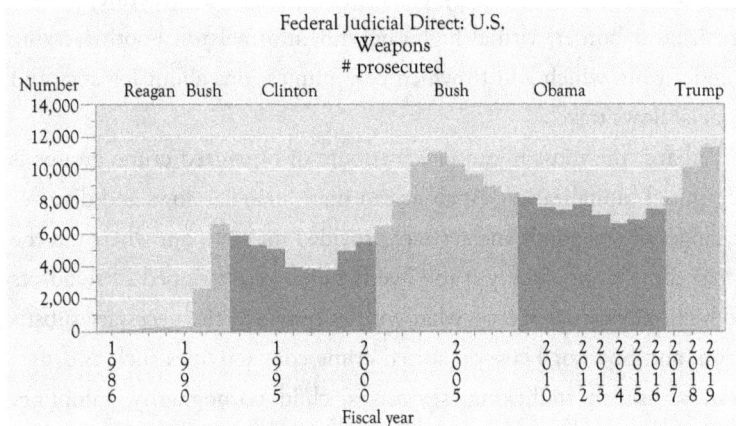

Figure 15.2 Federal weapons prosecutions, fiscal years 1986–2019

Source: Transactional Records Access Clearinghouse at Syracuse University (TRACfed)

measured by these prosecutions, is waning or undetected. The prosecution of underlying core offenses like drug and firearms distributions do not correlate with the organized crime prosecutions.

In fact, if organized crime as conceived, theorized, and prosecuted by the U.S. law enforcement were the source of many social harms, the significant decline in organized crime prosecutions would suggest that

Federal Judicial District: U.S.
Organized Crime
prosecuted

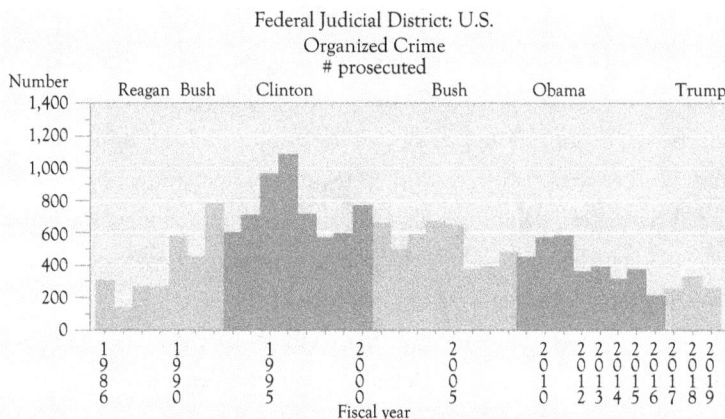

Figure 15.3 Federal organized crime prosecutions, fiscal years 1986–2019

Source: Transactional Records Access Clearinghouse at Syracuse University (TRACfed)

a different source(s) is responsible for the persistent predicate crime offenses such as importation of drugs and exportation of firearms. These glocal criminal acts are not committed by rogue individuals but through organizational structures different from those conceived traditionally such as entrepreneurial and opportunistic matrices and networks discussed herein. However, from the activity of federal prosecutors, it would seem that organized crime was conquered but the constituent criminal activities continue independently.

In brief, core organized crime activities were not monopolized by groups such as the five families. These groups did not in fact form an influential cartel like the organization of petroleum exporting countries (OPEC); though they were not bit players, the leadership was more notorious and infamous than necessary and significant to the worldwide supply and demand inherent to organized crime activities.

While the public sector generally and law enforcement agencies specifically have experienced mixed successes with respect to the minimization of the risks and harms incident to glocal organized crime groups, there seems widely shared agreement as to what is required to mitigate the hazards presented by such criminal matrices: The financial and analytical capacities of law enforcement agencies need development (Council of

Europe 2015, p. 21). Organized crime groups thrive on exploiting this vulnerability of criminal investigators, public prosecutors, and regulatory agencies. These control agencies in the public and independent (e.g., non governmental organizations) sectors are not as prepared as they could and should be. The criminal network obtains, moves, secretes, and disguises financial resources, including bulk cash and electronic money, such that only a well-coordinated, globally focused counter-group of detective and preventive control mechanisms can meet the challenges.

However, this is not to suggest that focus on an abstract conception of organized crime groups as a global phenomenon exclusively demands transnational or cross-border solutions. Problems incident to organized criminal activity begin in response to local conditions. Networks form from the connections between groups and individuals locally (Hobbs and Dunnighan 1998, 298). Thus, the structure of an organized criminal group is grounded in and developed from the socio economic conditions of the specific locality. These attendant circumstances nurture the creation, persistence, evolution, and even dissolution of organized criminal activity. The question is "what are present and absent in the local community that contribute to organized criminal activity?"

The theory that a strong state can quash organized crime is in a sense plausible. However, this changes the conditions on the ground such that other forms of organized crime may evolve (e.g., corruption of public officials, private commercial bribery, legislation favoring special interests at the expense of the general welfare). A strong state may be particularly vulnerable to organized economic exploitation that, while causing significant public harm, is technically neither criminal nor unlawful. The crime may be what is legal.

State controls and emergency powers put in place in response to alleged threats posed by organized crime groups may be pretextual, especially where details about such groups are sparse and speculative. Extension of state power may be obtained under exaggerated threats of organized criminal activities; this extension may be used not only to further state interests in support of special interests (e.g., mining operations, deforestation, agriculture) but to suppress local protest (Papadovassilakis 2020). Organized crime groups have historically and recently provided the skeleton for a frightening boogeyman to convince the uninformed public at large of the great need for the implementation of potent control mechanisms available to law enforcement and national intelligence agencies (e.g., mass surveillance). The larger question remains: has the fear of transnational organized crime been inflated for reasons that have little to do with staunching illicit importing and exporting of contraband?

In a sense, glocal demands too much from governments. To interpret and analyze the organized criminal group as a functioning unit analogous to a publicly filing corporation with subsidiaries, divisions, and fixed company agents across the globe is to miss the dynamic aspect of the organized criminal group: it arises from deficient local socio economic conditions by exploiting the vulnerabilities of individuals seeking extralegal means to accomplish their objectives. For example, U.S. college admissions may be corrupted by small groups of individuals, including consultants, college officials, parents, and students, to obtain special consideration. Where the stakes are high and access and acceptance can be purchased, this fact pattern will recur.

Without a sense of proportion and humility, the analyst will not conceive of the essential properties of organized crime—how these morph and persist contingent on existing and readily created opportunity structures notwithstanding whether the host country is "developed, emerging, or undeveloped." Gaming the rules depends on the specific rules, and all rules in human affairs can be gamed (except the rule that there are no rules!). The policymaker can wrongheadedly allow him- or herself to become enmeshed in and dependent on a misleading paradigm. While stronger connections among organized criminals are local, transient and fluid connectivity characterize global relationships. Thus, there is a deep offshore bench for replacing international participants and facilitators.

Often, governments' priorities ebb and flow, depending on their current leadership and its perceptions of public opinions, which are more often manipulable and myopic than fixed and persistent in expressed preferences. Organized crime can appear as formidable as the instruments of media depict, or it may seem a problem largely solved by modern law enforcement techniques, including the deployment of deep and wide electronic surveillance tools. For example, after the 9/11 attacks in the United States, investigative and intelligence priorities were shifted dramatically (U.S. Department of Justice Office of the Inspector General 2004, ii).

Like many public policy issues, the measurement of the threat of organized crime is left to experts such as criminologists, economists, sociologists, and other social scientists. They aggregate and interpret the data to be used, usually statistics prepared by a bureaucracy within the government, according to quantitative models using regression analysis, surveys, and sources that are unauditable. Dependent variables may include the level of organized crime convictions per capita, and independent variables may include society wide demographic data. The substance and quality of Inferences are debatable.

Undoubtedly, the models developed by social scientists using governmental data are flawed; however, the difficulty is how flawed? As in the dilemma faced by investors with respect to public companies that know some management assertions and some public auditor reports are invalid and unreliable—the objective uncertainty about distinguishing the valid and reliable from the invalid and unreliable creates more a predicament than a problem: it is not timely solvable with limited resources.

In 1970, the RICO Act was enacted in the United States, empowering the federal government and private parties to make both legitimate and illegitimate enterprises and their high managerial agents liable for criminal and unlawful activities. These criminal and civil actions are premised on the commission of a pattern of racketeering activity by any enterprise. Thus, sophisticated criminal networks could be disabled from the top-down (Blakey 1990, 879–80). With high penalties, including long prison terms and treble damage awards, the deterrent effect on organized crime seemed palpable.

Table 15.1 depicts a selected series of key data elements arising from the criminal investigation and public prosecution by the U.S. Department of Justice under the program category of organized crime. No data are available prior to 1986, and some data are not available until 1992.

In brief, the responsiveness to criminal referrals by criminal investigators (primarily, the Federal Bureau of Investigation) to public prosecutors (primarily, the district Offices of the United States Attorneys) seems fairly consistent for the period fiscal years 1986 through 2018. However, the increase in median prison terms over the past several years suggests that the gravity of harm committed by organized crime in the United States might have become more serious. Alternatively, only the punishments

Table 15.1 Criminal prosecutions under U.S. DoJ's organized crime program category

Organized Crime by Fiscal Year	No. of Prosecutions Filed	Percent of Referrals Prosecuted	Median Prison Term (in mos.)
1986	304	55	N/A
1989	264	50	N/A
1992	778	63	15
1995	965	66	8
1998	571	55	12
2001	659	58	15
2004	674	63	16
2007	393	60	23
2010	572	63	41
2013	390	56	42
2016	211	45	41
2018	333	59	41

Source: Data from Transactional Records Access Clearinghouse at Syracuse University (TRACfed)

became more severe. Nonetheless, the number of prosecutions at recent levels (i.e., post-2013) might suggest that the puzzle of organized crime control has been solved. Of course, the mystery of the persistence of core predicate criminal activities has not been resolved, with crimes such as drug and firearm distributions largely unaffected by organized crime prosecutions. The paradigm of organized crime as an output of the big evil man (e.g., Capone, Genovese, Gotti) is not helpful.

CHAPTER 16

Organized Crime and New Participants

The Internet is not a well-organized market dominated by fixed social norms. It is wide open and more anarchic than orderly. Generally, users are free to lie, create the foundations of illicit relationships, and often remain anonymous. The Internet is the software-hardware backbone of good things (e.g., scientific and scholarly collaboration) and bad things (e.g., conspiracies and antitrust collusion). Traditional organized crime arose before the invention of the Internet, and some have argued that the use of the Internet generally has resulted in an enhanced facilitation of criminal activities, for example, the Internet fosters cybercrime committed collectively whether globally and/or locally. However, it might not have created new groups of organized criminals as per the traditional hierarchical model (McCusker 2006, 273), but it has birthed transnational organized economic crime using legitimate and illegitimate pathways, for example:

- Transnational high tech organizations (e.g., Google, Twitter, Facebook) provide virtual meet-and-greet venues. These platforms do not conduct due diligence on their users; they do not audit and investigate the claims and aims of the users. Their collective expanse is a hybrid of wasteland and fecundity, for better and worse.
- PayPal and other fintech services create new opportunities to conduct licit and illicit financial flows among originators, intermediaries and correspondents, and beneficiaries. The natural persons directing, controlling, and benefiting from these opportunistic pathways are protected from transparency, disclosure, and accountability, often by rule of law.

Social media empowered through the Internet offers a fairly safe and efficient means for black and gray market participants to hook up and conspire, assuming the use of counter-surveillance software and hardware to confuse, mislead, and distract law enforcement and intelligence agencies. However, deeper, more clandestine pathways are available to obtain tools to create and exploit black and gray markets.

As no highly profitable, infamous crime is accomplished alone, collusion is necessary. Networks and associations of individuals are necessary to effectuate the processes of finding customers, providing goods and services, obtaining payments, and so on. This occurs in legitimate and illegitimate enterprises. However, the illicit nature of organized crime demands more circumspection than legitimate businesses that may advertise and promote liberally. Significantly, to a great extent, organized crime operates like a network economy (Wainwright 2016, 175): knowledge of, trust in, and anonymity of suppliers and customers outside of the network is necessary to avoid the web of law enforcement.

Analogous to legitimate businesses organized crime deploys and leverages high tech, including exploiting, for example, the capacities of the TOR (the onion router) browser to conceal the locations (Internet protocol addresses) of persons using the dark web's otherwise inaccessible websites (see Marker 2019). Anonymity breeds fraud and corruption as much as unbridled power and unchecked discretion foster abuse and lack of accountability, other things being equal. Thus, the inherent unaccountability and leverageable socioeconomic power from unchecked, unmonitored end-to-end encryption tend to corrupt, with the dark web, a key set of covert pathways to organize, commit, and conceal criminal activities.

The dark web is comprised of thousands of websites that can only be accessed with special browser software (e.g., Tor), facilitating illicit activity including transnational money laundering (Quintero 2017). Through anonymity, encryption, and the use of virtual currencies, users connecting with likeminded others to exchange goods, including child pornography, for monetary value (e.g., bitcoins) endeavor to act under the radar of law enforcement and intelligence agency surveillance. These conditions facilitate wrongful acts and their concealment, resulting in the expansion of successful opportunities for transnational organized crime. In brief, cryptocurrencies such as bitcoin and the dark web's menu of products and services may comprise a vehicle and pathway for fraud, arms dealing, and terrorism by organized crime (Georgetown Security Studies Review 2018).

In brief, the dark web is a virtual convergence point that functions as broker for buyers and sellers of illicit goods such as drugs, firearms, and cybercrime tools (e.g., malware) (Europol 2018). Software tools such as Tor and 12P would be deployed to access and exploit the dark web's goods and services offerings under cover of encryption. Additionally, the use of virtual private networks (VPNs) could be used to hide the fact that the user is deploying tools such as Tor or 12P; without a VPN, the user's internet service provider (ISP) would be aware that the user is using these tools. Together, tools such as Tor or 12P and working through a VPN empower both legitimate users seeking privacy and illegitimate users seeking to procure or sell illicit goods and services (Holden n.d.). Superficially, the market is neutral, neither necessarily white nor necessarily black/gray.

Thus, the dark web creates a big, covert store of information (a virtual mall) wherein illicit goods and services may be negotiated for purchase and sale with a level of anonymity that cannot be obtained through traditional worldwide web browsing inside the Internet. Organized criminal activity is facilitated through this computed-based intransparency, facilitating the development, persistence, and growth of gig-style entrepreneurial and clandestine networks—an encrypt-able "Uber" for illicit conduct.

The dark web fosters an underground virtual opportunistic economy where information can be obtained about potential accomplices and means and methods may be secured (Security Intelligence 2016). Outsourcing of key and necessary skills such as coding for cybercrime and fraud is accomplished efficiently and effectively through the dark web, empowering otherwise small groups or cells of criminal actors to leverage the severity and social harms of their actions and broaden their range of victims (e.g., banks through hacker coding and identity theft): the art of cyber-facilitated fraud and theft as a modern transnational gig.

Some salient observations:

- Criminal transactions using the computer characterize global networks and gigs. The computer bridges the physical separation and gives rise to activities that seem legit but are not (e.g., high quality forgeries and faked websites).

• The dark web, which exists beyond the searchable Internet used by mainstream scholars, analysts, and other users, comprises a criminogenic virtual venue wherein secrecy allows for shadowy conduct—ideal for gray and black markets.

• Tools for mitigating the risks presented by the dark web are most effective when (from the perspective of the United States) composed of partnerships of international, federal, state, local, tribal, and private sector organizations in an information sharing environment.

• Activities conducted through the dark web are inherently covert, in a sense, but they are not *ipso facto* illicit. Individuals may use the dark web to conduct white market transactions (e.g., joining social clubs) (Guccione 2020).

Cybercrime and security intelligence have been given significant attention at official agencies since September 11, 2001. Law enforcement agencies such as the U.S. Federal Bureau of Investigation and intelligence offices such as the U.S. Director of National Intelligence have combined forces in formal and informal partnerships with other key entities in the public and private sectors on a worldwide basis to corral the threat of transnational organized economic crimes committed through global webs of entrepreneurs using computer-based tools to communicate with one another, form alliances, obtain criminally others' identities and properties, and get away with these collective acts of theft, deceit, and, in some cases, terrorism support. However, the success of these official partnerships is unclear. See Figure 16.1 below.

The pattern seems familiar: officially pump up the threat level, using mass media and other experts, scholars, and analysts, to demand counterintelligence and risk mitigation strategies; obtain oodles of financial resources and funding from the governments; conduct widespread electronic surveillance and deployment of other investigative and intelligence tools (e.g., informants paid by law enforcement agencies) and/or elements of the intelligence community (e.g., the U.S. Central Intelligence Agency); prosecute criminal activities, where necessary. In brief, the trend

Federal Judicial: U.S.
Internal Security/Terrorism
prosecuted

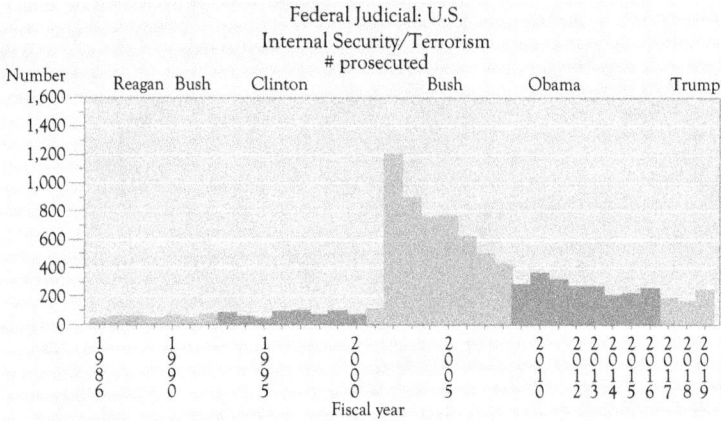

Figure 16.1 *Federal Internet security and terrorism prosecutions, fiscal years 1986–2019*

Source: Transactional Records Access Clearinghouse at Syracuse University (TRACfed)

of prosecutions indicates, consistent with the boosting of the threat of traditional organized crime, that the level of threat is not commensurate with criminal investigations and public prosecutions.

In a sense, the threat is invisible (which is not equivalent to denying that victims' identities are stolen, corporate treasuries and offerings of products and services are not subjected to denial of service attacks, and so on). Moreover, during these high times characterized by extensive signals intelligence and surveillance webs, it seems a wonder that anyone gets away with anything.

CHAPTER 17

Professions and the New Organized Crime: Control

The distinctions drawn between organized crime and white-collar crime may serve to obfuscate and neutralize the gravity of harms (e.g., organized crime as an illicit tool of ethnically related thugs and white-collar crime as a tool of financially sophisticated clerks and managers). A more accurate phrasing of organized crime, which includes many white-collar crimes such as securities fraud, would be the term "organized economic crime" (Vande Walle 2002, 289). This term better describes the nature of such coordinated criminal activity as the pursuit of profit and power through illicit means and methods. Criminal goals and objectives (e.g., the persistence of covert and outlawed enterprises embarking on exchanges of goods and services through markets—black, gray, or white) are, in a sense, theoretical. The score requires completion of the economic circuit, that is, procurement of liquid assets and political influence with which to sustain or enhance the participants' financial positions. Goods such as drugs and firearms are the instruments; criminal proceeds represent the penultimate stage. Real economic value is comprised of that which these proceeds may obtain (e.g., real estate, automobiles, health care).

In construing the concept of organized crime, it is essential not to underestimate the roles of representatives of business, law enforcement, and criminal justice (Woodiwiss 2017, 247–48). These critical facilitators participate in making organized crime effective both as to accomplishing its illicit goals and concealing the nature of its actual activities. That is, the criminal acts are laundered, often with the assistance of professionals such as lawyers, accountants, bankers, and company formation agents. Thus, it is necessary to use a practical working definition of organized crime that includes both its traditional interpretation (e.g., drugs and arms trafficking) and its white-collar crime aspect (e.g., financial crimes, fraud)

(Center for the Study of Democracy 2010, 27). As noted previously, transnational organized economic crime seems a phrase that encompasses the white, gray, and black market activities.

In a sense, gambling is at the heart of organized economic crime. The mathematical interest, emotional vesting, and potential for financial gain accruing from using games of chance to lure the upperworld into the underworld with gambling activities at the cusp and border have long been practically undeniable (Russo 2001, 505–06). Gambling offers both the well-capitalized and the undercapitalized the opportunity to increase exponentially one's financial resources. To the upperworld, it provides ancillary benefits (e.g., capturing consumers' attention to advertising media), and to the underworld, it provides highly leveraged profitability and power over the customer-victims, so long as the loan shark has an effective enforcement mechanism.

Of course, discussion and analysis of organized criminal enterprises and their attributes invariably leads to assessments of plausibility of narrative and credibility of source and even exhaustive studies such as those made by Russo and others are subject to disagreement by and among scholars (Lurigio and Binder 2013, 213) (see also, Lombardo 2013b, 297). Reaching truthful narrative demands more of the reasoning skills inherent in abduction than induction or deduction, with confidence always immeasurably less than certain. Abduction is a skill acquired through experience and skepticism, attributes that do not support a quick rise to the top of one's practice area, whether in academia or the professions.

While the tendency is to conceive of traditional organized crime as membership in a criminal enterprise and widespread conspiracy among individuals, the working definition of organized crime conceived herein includes the traditional gangs of extortion and extends its application to collusive acts of professionals and other so-called white-collar individuals that aid and abet the successful commission and concealment of street crimes such as prostitution and gambling, as well as boardroom crimes such as insider trading and market manipulation. The stress is less on the specific type of crime than on the means and methods used to commit and conceal the crime (i.e., high levels of coordination among individuals inside and outside of the formally defined enterprise, whether denoted the Gambino crime family or the Enron senior management team).

An essential means of concealing the nature of commercial activities and transactions is the use of complicated structuring of parties, counterparties, entities, and the transaction itself. This artificially imposed complexity effectively discourages tax and regulatory officials, law enforcement agencies, investigative journalists, and intelligence agencies from obtaining knowledge of financial flows, licit and illicit (Fitzgibbon and Hallman 2020). Professionals such as attorneys, wealth managers, accountants and auditors, and company formation agents facilitate the development of intentional intransparency. Opacity is not a bug; it is by design. This method of conducting transactions need not be the sole method of operation (e.g., illegitimate activities may hide behind and become aggregated into voluminous data of legitimate transactions, making discovery time-consuming, expensive, and often avoidable), but it is key to persistence of the (transnational) organized economic crime group.

While the primary method of operation of organized crime depends on violence, threats of violence, and intimidation to obtain criminal proceeds (with the victims' recourse to rules of law muted lest the unappealable death penalty be unilaterally imposed by mafia strongarms), success in concealment of the commission of organized crimes depends often on professionals, also known as the white collars (Cara 2015, 477). The white collars clean up and fix the legal issues that may arise, that is, they are the fixers and facilitators. They will assist in disguising the ill-gotten criminal gains as the fruits of legitimate business; attorneys, accountants, auditors, bankers, and others are essential for this process to work effectively. With their specialized knowledge and skills, criminal proceeds are laundered.

Thus, the professions are corrupted. Attorneys, accountants, bankers, financial advisors, and so on are used in the furtherance of illicit schemes of organized crime groups. The involvement may be purposeful (i.e., the professional seeks to collaborate and collude in the scheme by providing key facilitating services); knowing or reckless (i.e., the professional knows of or consciously disregards the risk of organized crime involvement in providing his/her services); negligent (i.e., the professional could and should know of the specific organized crime group risk associated with providing his/her services), or unwitting (i.e., the professional is honestly and innocently bamboozled). In short, the professional services are bent and corrupted to facilitate illicit objectives and enable means of concealment and commission from money laundering to shell company formation (Ott 2010, p. 378). Moreover, they may be highly financially and reputationally rewarded for doing so (unless they're caught!)

However, the legal tools available to combat the threat of organized crime (e.g., RICO Act in the United States) may not extend to the outside professional service providers such as outside counsel, external auditors, and independent bankers who do not participate in the operations and management of the criminal enterprise (McCarthy 2019, 464–65). This, of course, illustrates the power of the gig organized crime structure—a network of independent contractors under a loose confederation with shared criminal objectives in the factual sense but not quite reaching the level of rigid hierarchical oversight commonly required in proving the existence of an overarching criminal enterprise. Thus, there are component units (nodes) within an ill-defined criminal enterprise (tenuous threads creating a gossamer web).

Each individual and node strives to maintain a patina of plausible deniability lest law enforcement or regulators pry too deeply and widely. In an important sense, organized crime represents a problematic preparation of books and records and failure to implement effective internal controls that results in corrupt collective practices. Disclosure of real transactions is fraudulent.

Notwithstanding the advantages of compartmentalization of the criminal enterprise, certain outside services are essential to preserve its influence, protect its profits and proceeds, and assure its persistence. Effective criminal enterprises need the law, too. The rule of law can be used to maintain secrecy of bank records, force investigative agencies to obtain warrants with cause (not whim), extend property rights to legitimate downstream/upstream businesses and personal residences, and so on. Attorneys, accountants, auditors, bankers, information technology professionals, and others perform necessary services to sustain criminal enterprises, sometimes knowingly, sometimes unwittingly, however, usually profitably.

Attorney, Accountants, Auditors, Bankers, Brokers, IT Professionals, et al.

Overall, the trend line for U.S. (federal) prosecutions of white collar crime has largely ebbed since fiscal year 1995. See Figure 17.1 below.

Federal Judicial District: U.S.
White Collar Crime
prosecuted

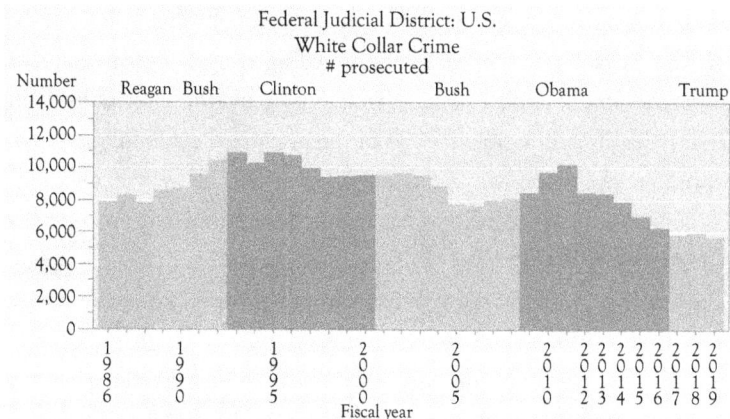

Figure 17.1 Federal white collar crime prosecutions, fiscal years 1986–2019

Source: Transactional Records Access Clearinghouse at Syracuse University (TRACfed)

Thus, it would seem the problem of white collar crime has been solved, and the focus analyzed in parts herein on organized economic crime should be redirected. That is plausible, but this author has yet to observe any theory or set of concepts that would explain the trend of increasing white collar integrity. Have attendant circumstances changed to constrict the opportunity structure for white collar crimes? Alternatively, the failure of white collar criminal prosecutions to climb may be attributable to disinterest among the senior federal prosecutorial and investigative class of high managerial agents in the public sector (i.e., decision makers and policymakers in their respective domains).

In brief, the rule of law may be overestimated with respect to general deterrence (cf. scapegoating to scare others) and specific deterrence (cf. non-prosecution and deferred prosecution leniency programs) for various categories of criminal activities.

Having talented (but amoral) attorneys is an essential attribute for organized economic crime. Without the specialized knowledge and skill to direct financial flows from domestic sources (e.g., sales of drugs and firearms) to offshore jurisdictions of safety and secrecy (e.g., Bahamas), the illicit enterprise would not persist. Knowing how to manipulate through the rules of law to clean up dirty sources into legitimate financial resources is a needed skill (Russo 2006, 526–27). Crafty lawyering empowers the criminal enterprise such that where successful over an extended period, the value of financial resources originally obtained through illicit means dwarfs the surface criminal activities of selling drugs, firearms, and so on. Imagine an inverted iceberg characterized by the enormous (and apparently legitimate) visible savings of the organized economic criminal enterprise in the upperworld fed period-over-period by the nefarious illegal and invisible schemes hidden below in the underworld. Growth may be exponential.

The attorney not only protects in the sense of functioning as a device to prevent law enforcement from arresting the key participants or seizing the criminal proceeds, but also functions as an architect in arranging the legal structure of entities strategically placed in the global network of (illicit) financial flows. The attorney helps make the illicit enterprise look legit.

While the role of accountants in discovering illicit financial transactions and providing assistance in criminal financial investigations (e.g., on behalf of the FBI) is well established, the complexity of modern business arrangements and globally distributed financial transactions make it even more essential that accountancy and accountants be deployed in addressing the risk of organized crime influence (Wolverton 2012). Accountants may be especially useful in the concealment and disguising of illicit transactions such that these appear to be legitimate. The accountant has the specialized knowledge of interpreting books and records into financial statements and reports, and generally accepted accounting principles (GAAP) are not self-executing. The accountant assists the principal organized crime figures in not only maintaining an accurate set of books summarizing who owes how much to whom but in creating a plausible scenario of legitimacy (see del Bosque 2017).

The accountant has the professional knowledge and skill to assist in the management of accruals to periodic statements and reports of revenues and expenses necessary to transform cash basis records in apparent accord with generally accepted accounting principles (GAAP). The accruals (adjusting journal entries to the books and records) provide a smokescreen of patent legitimacy, concealing, among other criminal objectives, tax evasion, money laundering, financing of terrorism, trafficking in humans, drugs, and firearms, and so on (Ravenda, Valencia-Silva, Argiles-Bosch, and Garcia-Blandon 2018, 309).

From the perspective of the criminal investigator, the accountant could have specialized knowledge (e.g., proper documentation of audit trail) and skills (e.g., sifting through volumes of data inherent in enhanced technology, including computers, cell phones, and so on) not common enough among traditional investigators (Quan 2019). Moreover, accountants often have the necessary expertise in gathering, documenting, organizing, and presenting evidence relevant to not only criminal activities committed to obtain illicit financial flows but criminal activities in support of layering and integrating these criminal proceeds in money laundering transactions (Monterrosa-Yancy 2017). Often, this expertise is developed while working on criminal investigations on behalf of the public prosecutor(s), resulting in the required know-how to prove allegations through evidence admissible in courts of law.

The perception of organized crime as brawn in lieu of brain (e.g., threats of violence and not sophisticated frauds) is mistaken (Cooper 2019). Accountants, along with lawyers and computer (information technology) experts, play a key role as apparently legitimate facilitators, enabling organized crime's success.

Additionally, forensic accountants (and forensic auditors) may work undercover in furtherance of criminal investigations on behalf of government agencies like the FBI or IRS (Drew 2015). Generally, these investigative accountants and fraud examiners use financial documentation such as bank records to assist in the organization and presentation of a federal criminal case to the district/task force United States Attorney's Office designated public prosecutor (e.g., the conviction of the purported Bonnano crime family boss Joseph Massino, FBI 2005).

Whether operating from the inside-out (e.g., accountant facilitator of crime, undercover criminal investigator) or the outside-in (e.g., forensic accountant/auditor, financial investigator), the knowledge and skills of accountancy offer much to the perpetrators and prosecutors. The successful commission and persistence of organized crime demands the implementation of sophisticated recordkeeping systems that are both accurate and covert as to the real commercial purposes of the enterprise. These records are used to measure and track financial flows and debits and credits of transactions (e.g., who owes how much to whom?) The accounting information system (AIS) must be comprehensive and clandestine (e.g., special codes) such that others cannot readily glean the illicit underlying purposes of the transactions.

The AISs may be enhanced through the knowledge and skills of experts in computer-based technologies, including encryption techniques. Thus, it is not unusual to find individuals with expertise in accountancy and digital technologies working together on the inside or the outside in furtherance of organized crime endeavors or in prosecution of organized crime, respectively. In brief, accounting expertise (i.e., knowledge and skill in financial accountability and AISs) may transform organized crime into a geographically wide, coordinated enterprise, without which centralization of power and direction would be difficult to maintain persistently. Moreover, accountants may facilitate the concealment of transactions, rendering financial reports such as tax returns both highly unreliable and a tool for law enforcement agents to unravel the hidden schemes of the enterprise and use as evidence of deceit.

Thus, accountants can readily facilitate the substantive commission of the crime of tax evasion and the substantive criminal concealment inherent to money laundering under a widespread, global criminal conspiracy (Tokar 2020b). From concealing beneficial owners to making shell companies seem legitimate, the accountant is key to spinning bogus reports, including financial statements and tax returns, from misleading records, including data of ownership of investments, funds, financial flows, and accounts.

Of course, the best organized economic and financial "crime" may be that which is lawful. Legitimately established commercial global enterprises have shifted billions upon billions of profits to low- or no-tax jurisdictions (i.e., tax havens such as the British Overseas Territories including Bermuda, the Cayman Islands, and the British Virgin Islands) that were earned in higher tax jurisdictions in which the enterprises derived most of their sales revenues (Tax Justice Network 2020). A particularly abusive tax evasion/avoidance scheme implicates the use of intellectual property (e.g., copyrights, patents) by which transfer pricing among affiliated entities is determined by the taxpayer so as to protect pre-tax income from the reach of tax administrations in the jurisdictions generating the revenue (Sterling 2019).

The investigator should not forget that corporations are formed in material part to limit liability. This includes tax liabilities and personal accountability. Corporations cannot be jailed (though legally in the United States, they have free speech; see *Citizens United v. Federal Elections Commission* 2010).

Auditors, including tax preparers and examiners and forensic accountants, play a key role in concealing and discovering organized criminal activity (see Raab 2005, 665). They can discover or not discover the reality of the economic transactions, contingent upon their abilities (e.g., are they hired because of their incompetency?) and their motivations (e.g., are they compensated way higher for fortressing plausible deniability rather than contributing to accuracy, completeness, and timeliness of financial reporting?)

Access to oodles of financial resources presents both the opportunity for lawful and the opportunity for unlawful gains. While many bankers are undoubtedly engaged in legitimate and socially desirable conduct, and few, if any, organized crime figures may be seen as legitimate actors in the political economy, there are hybrid organizations that while not criminal *per se* may properly be seen as criminogenic, for example, hedge funds (Stout 2010). The bridge between lawful and unlawful activity may be merely an opportunity away. Private investment vehicles pooling many investors' financial resources into offshore custodians and administrators using numbered or straw man accounts can readily facilitate illicit financial flows.

Likely, there exists a criminogenic ladder representative of the organized crime influence and forms in a given society: at rung one, there is found the legitimate business as victim of organized criminal activities (e.g., extortion, bid rigging); at rung two, there is found the hybrid business as cooperative with organized crime (e.g., labor racketeering and other improper influence over organized labor, money laundering services); at rung three, there is found an informal alliance between organized crime groups and public authorities, which comprises the most corrupt relationship (e.g., bribes, kickbacks) (Lars and Larsson 2011, 538).

Indeed, there are many commonalities among organized crime group loan-sharking, legitimate merchants, and quasi-governmental and private sector financial services institutions, including using issuance of debt as a tool to obtain fees (upon origination), income (interest), gains (capital), and assets (recovery of collateral). Loan sharking is unlawful, but the legal process defining the rights and obligations of creditors and debtors may bring about similar results (but for the leg-breaking) (Pistor 2020). Predation may be lawfully enabled.

Also, the decision to pursue a criminal inquiry may be all that distinguishes mafia-related frauds and so-called legitimate business enterprise frauds. That the police or criminal investigative agency may believe sufficient competent evidence exists from which to pursue a criminal action is not sufficient. The designated public prosecutor (immunized from second-guessing and other accountability mechanisms by prosecutorial discretion) calls the shots (Chapman 2020). Evidence on the ground may not move the public prosecutor (sometimes, the criminal investigator, also) to the most severe administrative action such as criminal charges. Professional discretion is usually opaque and transformative (i.e., the illicit transaction passes as licit due to inaction and material omission by the (ir)responsible high managerial agents in the criminal justice system).

Occasionally, it is difficult to determine who learns from whom: is organized crime teaching Wall Street or vice versa (Taibbi 2012)? Bid rigging, whether facilitated by brokers and capital providers or organized crime street thugs and loan sharks, is collusive criminal activity that is quintessentially white-collar financial fraud. Calling it white-collar Wall Street driven criminal conduct does not alter the required illicit cooperation among market participants to fleece victims (e.g., municipalities issuing bonds and parking proceeds). Racketeering and stock fraud may partner well together, facilitating boiler room operations and other manipulative practices (e.g., pump and dump schemes) infecting capital markets with organized crime (Weiser 1997). The white market is not pure; the gray market is ambiguous, and the black market is hidden.

To date, reliance has been placed upon the banking (and related) industry to identify suspicious transactions, including links to organized crime activities. This approach is inferior to the development and nurturance of global partnerships across the private and public sectors—banks and regulators (Schenck 2017). Domestic and international task forces may together provide a more effective detective control over transnational organized crime rather than excessive reliance on any given bank's internal control system. Indeed, cooperation in inspection and oversight is essential to overcome collusion in criminal activity.

While it would be foolhardy to denounce investigative strategies at the administrative (regulatory), civil, and criminal levels that elevate the principle of following the money, the reality is that the problem is significantly broader and deeper. Financial flows may be documented inaccurately, incompletely, and/or not adequately timely to allow a robust detective control (e.g., public auditors). In brief, the transaction's stated business purpose may be materially misleading but not apparent upon superficial inspection and oversight. Forensic auditors are not often tasked; the routine inspection and oversight is performed by public auditors.

Brokers may provide an essential service as intermediaries between sellers and buyers. Often, they work for commissions (e.g., skimming a percentage of the insured's premium payable as commission income). This commercial model is particularly applicable to organized crime's revenue streams: From loansharking to gambling to firearms/drugs trafficking, the illicit network is configured to deliver goods and services to buyers as an alternative pathway from the market norms. This is advantageous for the criminal organizations in many respects, including the ability to evade formal tax administration regimes imposed by the governing authorities.

Additionally, the provision of brokerage services is especially useful as an artifice to conceal illicit activities: Whether the services are entirely or partly fictitious is not often readily resolvable by reference to observable inputs. For example, finders' fees may be supported by associated travel and entertainment documentation, e-mails, telephone records, contracts, and so on, but the actual services provided may be disguised in material respects: the counterparties may not be at arm's length; the valuation of the services in the transaction may be grossly inflated, circumstances particularly helpful where there is a criminal objective of money laundering.

Briefly, the socially accepted, widespread use of (il)legal fictions (e.g., corporations, shell companies, holding companies, storefronts, one-person limited liability companies) under which to conduct transactions involving flows of monetary resources (or the rights thereto) across the globe almost instantaneously leaves much space for fraud, corruption, abuse, and other indicia of organized crime effects.

The commission of organized criminal activities, their concealment from law enforcement agencies, the laundering of criminal proceeds for personal and commercial uses, and the detection of these illicit activities implicates dependence on the knowledge and skills of information technology (IT) professionals. That is, perpetrating and detecting organized criminal networks through information and communications technology (ICT) is a modern cat-and-mouse game. Alleged encryption, security, and confidentiality are not absolute notwithstanding technical expertise deployed by the illicit network. For example, the global phone network France-based company EncroChat, which catered to organized crime drug and firearms traffickers in the UK and Europe, was apparently hacked by French law enforcement authorities to eavesdrop over months on a multitude of electronic communications previously believed confidential and private by the organized criminals (Cox 2020). During the three-month operation centered on EncroChat, hundreds were arrested, including two law enforcement officers. EncroChat had approximately 60,000 subscribers (Shaw 2020).

Canada-based Phantom Secure was also an encrypted communication service, having been taken down by the Federal Bureau of Investigation (FBI) in March 2018 (FBI News 2018). At least six law enforcement agencies across the globe—from North America to Asia—were involved in the dissolution of this ICT service dedicated to the facilitation and concealment of transnational organized criminal enterprises.

The old saw about living and dying by the sword may be applied analogously to the ICT boasting of secure, uncompromisable communication platforms and services. The difficulty of verifying the bona fides of such IT sellers is not insurmountable but not remotely transparent. Moreover, the risk that a given seller is a front or otherwise infected and controlled by law enforcement cannot be underestimated. Thus, the organized crime network undoubtedly demands a high level of enhanced dark due diligence; that is, the means and methods of establishing trustworthiness both as to the quality of the products and services offered and to the willingness and capacity of the controlling persons to commit to secretive engagement in the (wink-and-nod) support of organized criminal activities are not within the scope of routine due diligence providers. Darkness hides corruption.

The business model of the broker supports the gig political economies—licit and illicit. The broker, as neither an owner-dealer of contraband or prohibited services maintains the illusion of clean hands. He or she does not carry an inventory; plausible deniability is preserved. The broker can readily mime legitimacy. Moreover, the objects brokered (e.g., financial products, insurance, real estate) are often high-valued, facilitating the efficient and effective movement of unlawful proceeds.

In practice, the criminal investigation of organized crime groups is impaired by a lack of sophisticated IT. The availability of a structured and efficient database that is widely cross-referenced across the ICT of criminal investigative units through cross-border jurisdictions is necessary to detect, monitor, and prepare for prosecution the actors involved in organized (and unorganized) crime. The level and usefulness of IT may determine who wins the battles—organized criminals or law enforcement agencies (Fisher and Quinto Elemento Lab 2020). Applications enhancing the usefulness of video evidence, especially facial recognition technologies, offer great potential for law enforcement (with attendant threats to individual privacy that should not be ignored).

Briefly, it may be fairly concluded that information technology, including the provision of high tech means of creating and distributing messages, arranging virtual conferences, and facilitating collaborative and coordinated decision making, is essential to the maintenance and growth of modern networked organized crime groups, which can presently obtain and deliver the professional and specialized services of ICT expertise on a global basis (Nicola and Scartezzini 2000, 346).

Other professionals such as casino operators and company formation agents sometimes provide material assistance to the preservation and growth of both transnational organized crime and transnational organized economic activity that resembles, but for the overall lack of coordinating interest of criminal investigators, public prosecutors, and leadership within the political economies of so many jurisdictions, organized crime (e.g., antitrust activity).

Organized crime infiltration of legitimate business is nefarious and subtle, however associations between targets of criminal investigations and participation in the governance structure of legitimate businesses may be established, justifying the need for effective monitoring of the C-suite (i.e., executive management) and board of directors, as well as strict scrutiny of relationships between private sector companies and the public sector generally (e.g., regulators, law enforcement agencies, judges, prosecutors) (Mirenda, Mocetti, and Rizzica 2019). Transnational organized economic activities, whether formally denoted a crime (bribery and kickbacks) or informally considered socially harmful (e.g., outsourcing and externalizing pollution in a global regulatory race to the bottom), comprise a high level threat to markets and residents on a worldwide basis. The compartmentalization of inspection and oversight, including regulation, law enforcement, and intelligence services, to local, state, and even federal levels is a vulnerability exploited both by high managerial agents in the political economy and by lower level facilitators and participants networked transnationally. These administrative, preventive, detective control activities need to be coordinated strategically at the worldwide level.

The white market, to the extent it exists and can be positively differentiated, has been infected and integrated with the unlawful activities practiced in the gray and black markets.

CHAPTER 18

The Future of Organized Crime

Organized criminal networks are here to stay for the short- and medium-, if not long-terms, unless radical transformations occur. The incentives of unlawful activities are great and lure both the desperately vulnerable and merely insecure. Thus, the future of organized crime will resemble the past, especially where the role of global banking is concerned. In brief, global banking facilitates more than prevents and detects, independently of whether the analyst focuses on the United States or on offshore financial institutions. The financial services sector has been corrupted in many respects (Fitzgibbon 2020).

Moreover, the rule of law under unchecked prosecutorial discretion is inadequate as an administrative control over organized crime as deal-making and the mindset of "the law means what I say it means" (cf. Humpty Dumpty) approach by the offices of public prosecutors, especially in the United States, allow careerism and corruption to continue without transparency and accountability (Koehler 2020). The problem undefined grows malignantly.

Without effective accounting and administrative controls operative throughout society, especially in the private sector's financial services and real estate industries and in the public sector's legislative and executive branches, transnational organized economic crime and its corrupting effects will persist and expand in breadth across jurisdictions and in depth in firms' operations, investment, and finance activities.

Indeed, it's difficult to get leadership among the richest political economies to coordinate efforts. It may very well be that getting someone to understand something against his or her financial and socioeconomic class interests is beyond the influence of impartial and empathetic reasoning (cf. Lombardi 2019 [quoting Upton Sinclair]). Profitability and self-interest trumping the general welfare and social weal.

Where there is significant capacity to organize (e.g., through the Internet and dark web using sophisticated information and communications technology) and globally founded willingness to organize (e.g., so many desperate and precarious lives without adequate licit opportunities), the emergence of transnational organized economic crime groups should surprise no one.

Fundamentally, under capitalism (i.e., private ordering and decision making about the structure of opportunities in the political economy) and the (neo)liberal political economy, profitability, gain, and influence are paramount goals such that competition among and exploitation of the vulnerable are the norm (i.e., rules *de jure* such as employment at will in the United States) and practice (i.e., *de facto* procedures such as the monetization of public goods and services). In a sense, truly pervasive organized crime would include rules of law supporting exploitative conditions in the legal framework of the jurisdiction beyond the merely technical limitations applicable to specifically denoted criminal acts, agreements, and enterprises imposed by the formal definition of organized crime (Lloyd A. 2020, 91). That is, the legalization of exploitation would obviate the need for much of what passes as organized crime, leaving in remainder a society and political economy where only the elite (e.g., law- and policy makers, captains of industry) thrive, and the non-elite compete vigorously and ceaselessly against one another for spoils.

Perhaps, this is where we are: a globalized opportunity structure in which informal alliances—gig-like in nature—define much of non-elite transnational organized crime, with the elite at practical liberty of creating formal transnational organized economic enterprises beyond the rule of law of any specific jurisdiction; of any specific regulatory agency, or of any specific public sector administration.

Organized crime is private ordering and private command-and-control, operating extralegally where the rule of law cannot be co-opted and corrupted.

Moreover, the corruption of the public sector is not unusual such that abuse of the formal rules of law is widespread, resulting in compromises of the public interest, including the provision of intelligence services and deployment of surveillance technology for the purpose of benefiting organized criminal networks (Salomon, Avalos, and Asmann

2020). It is not enough merely to have laws prohibiting some acts punishable as organized crime. The scope of rules of law, including their enforcement and punishment practices, needs to support public values such as transparency, integrity, accountability, honesty and fair dealing, and so on. An excessive dedication to private property and confidentiality of ownership and control structures over private property support transnational organized economic crime, elevating inadequately checked private interests over public interests, and the general welfare.

Where profit, gain, and personal power are high and superseding priorities, there develops an invisible race to the ethical bottom that includes the practice of organized illegal (including criminal) activities in the formal and informal political economies. Where the physical public works and software tools and techniques (e.g., the Internet and other computer-based information and communications technologies have created a form of white, gray, and dark global electronic villages), the factual means and methods dwarf national capacities to prevent, discover, and punish wrongful conduct. Ours is a world wherein corporations, including shells and fronts, are inherently persons (unless proven fraudulent), and locations of accounts and funds are lawfully attributed to financial institutions and service providers' addresses (e.g., a bank in the Cayman Islands may be the custodian for an account or fund that is effectively controlled by an undisclosed individual residing on Park Avenue, New York).

The Kafkaesque legal separation of form and substance practiced worldwide, especially in the United States, is the grand loophole. Thus, even small organizations of motivated affluent individuals can materially offshore their assets and income; their collective power in the political economies in which they reside have stripped domestic legal authorities of the ability to meaningfully, timely, accurately, and completely affix and associate their properties with their residencies, specifically shrinking tax bases and generally debilitating the general welfare. Beneficial control is hidden in the labyrinthine underworld, with the materially misleading upperworld comprised of legally owned trust accounts, funds, and legal costumes about which the public at large, law enforcement agencies, and regulators are largely ignorant.

Given that deep and extensive knowledge about organized crime is more analytical than descriptive and more abstract than concrete, the tendency to generalize with absolutes should be avoided in theorizing and conceiving how organized crime develops, persists, shrinks, and morphs into other formations (Von Lampe 2016, 336). What is reliably known is dwarfed by what can and will be. Organized criminal groups and their activities are structures and processes in transition, depending on external opportunities in the local, regional, and global political economies and on internal social skills of individuals that coalesce into organized crime groups. Heterogeneity among individuals with access to networks and markets rules over homogeneity such as shared ethnicity that characterized mythical and actual constructs of the Sicilian mafia.

Moreover, the tools with which to facilitate organized criminal activities, especially computer-based information and communications technology, demand new coalitions among the tech savvy, those with access to the underworld, and those that can further the objectives of concealment of the illicit activity and conversion of the proceeds into apparently legitimate accounts within licit financial institutions such as lawyers, bankers, and accountants. The underworld works hand-in-glove with the upperworld.

If one were to imagine, simplistically perhaps but not materially misleading, the state of organized criminal activities currently dominant in the world, it would be a transactional system using the U.S. dollar as the (electronic) functional currency, with enormous volumes of cash outflows from the United States arising from domestic drug purchases and enormous volumes of cash inflows to the United States arising from international arms sales—this circuit comprises the bread-and-butter of transnational organized economic crime today. Of course, other meals are served (e.g., human trafficking, gambling, purchasing of political favors), too.

If one were to codify the rules *de facto* of organized crime development, they would be as follows:

1. Limit information and communications on a need to know basis (i.e., practice discretion or perish; commit violence and deploy extortionate means);
2. Mimic the outward conduct of licit commercial enterprise (e.g., use offshore corporations and trusts; use lawfully established global banking and other financial services providers);

3. Strive to make the illicit licit (e.g., bribes and illegal gratuities become campaign contributions and independent expenditures; the scope of official misconduct and proscribing of dishonest services is narrowed through legal technicalities at supreme levels).

In brief, the covert gig and secretive network grow and become legit (cf. bootlegging in prohibition-era United States to lawful distilleries of today), first by obtaining the cooperation of the desperate and vulnerable, then by co-opting commercial enterprises, and finally by exercising political clout in branches of government. When organized crime groups reach critical mass, they become transnational organized economic "crime" groups, with the definition of "crime" limited as far as influence will permit.

The key mediator variable that empowers the development of transnational organized economic crime is the practice of divorcing an entity's formal registration space from its transactions space, that is, it conducts licit and illicit business far and wide away from where it is technically found, notwithstanding the comparatively tenuous and trivial relationship between transactions responsible for profits, gains, and influence and registrations controlling the so-called locus of the accounts and funds at issue. By way of illustration, the post office addresses of entities, including financial institutions and investors' trusts, in Georgetown, Cayman Islands create an evasive and false front to the world, reflecting a decision to choose light touch regulation over heavy touch supervision in the inspection and oversight of globally organized transactions (cf. take the money from consumers and victims and run to tax and secrecy havens).

It is not sufficient to have the willingness and capacity to commit the organized criminal activities. There needs to be an opportunity structure permitting concealment activities that don't raise the so-called red flags (e.g., the use of lawfully formed shell or holding corporations in tax havens) and allow easy and quick (electronic) access to the financial resources held in licit financial institutions (e.g., correspondent and private banking). The upperworld creates opportunity, whether deliberately or recklessly through defectively designed legislation (e.g., tax administrations that lack the resources and commitment to enforce evenhandedly the tax laws and regulations), or worse—through the corruption of investigative and prosecutorial decision making driven more by careerist-minded criminal investigators and public prosecutors seeking their next gig than by public servants committed to criminal justice as a public interest mission notwithstanding the potentially biasing power of influential patrons and cronies in the political economy.

The opportunity structure within the political economy has been reformed by a rules-based culture comprised primarily of demands for compliance with legislative and regulatory initiatives—a top-down approach. These operate by rooting out organized crime groups through formalized and routinized disclosure. This checklist type of approach has been called crime proofing the opportunity (Calderoni 2015, 131). Based entirely on the empirical decrease in public prosecutions of organized crime in the United States, it may be deemed apparently successful. Moreover, one cannot seriously argue against requests for disclose notwithstanding the inefficacy of such preventive control measures, yet transparency and accountability problems in both the upperworld in relation to itself and the upperworld in relation to the underworld have not been remotely solved.

Full and fair disclosure requirements made within the underworld in relation to itself are removed from upperworld limitations: where one's range of options includes murder, extortion, and deceit changes in rules of law are, in a sense, feckless.

New sins and criminogenic opportunities evolve from regulatory gaps and loopholes in the imperfect system of rule of law. The structure and culture of organized crime as a means of extracting financial resources from others persist informally as a perennial problem for the criminal justice system (Karstedt, Levi, and Godfrey 2006, 974). The present opportunity structure does not adequately mitigate the risk of organized economic crime formation at either domestic or international levels. High tech enhances the means and methods of organizing (e.g., separation space is shrunk), and digital currencies enhance the liquidity of criminal proceeds (e.g., money velocity is increased). Time, also, is compressed: one can obtain criminally sourced funds rapidly and transform their character nearly instantaneously in the global village, which is vast geographically but intimate technologically.

The convergence of the white, gray, and black markets (e.g., producers and distributors of lawful and unlawful goods and services, facilitators, financiers, and investment professionals providing lawful and unlawful asset protection scheme products and services) is criminogenic. Opportunities overlap between the upper- and underworlds: rate of return on investment trumps compliance with rule of law, especially where rule of law may be corrupted (e.g., bribes, kickbacks, campaign contributions, independent expenditures indirectly in support of candidates for political office, shell companies, tax havens and tax secrecy jurisdictions, lack of disclosure regarding beneficial ownership of accounts, funds, and trusts, and so on).

Moreover, the state of self-regulation and firm-wide efforts to control transnational organized economic crime is deficient (e.g., weak compliance among global money centers to ferret out, prevent, and contribute to the punishment of money laundering). Routine controls (e.g., automated review of transaction detail) and nonroutine controls (e.g., selected cases for further investigation) comprise window dressing to cover lightly transnational organized economic criminal activities. Customers, clients, intermediaries, facilitators and other white market participants, as well as regulatory and supervisory agencies, may readily be spoofed by gray and black market participants; this fraudulent mimicry of legitimacy is essential for successful criminal endeavors.

The regimes imposed under rules of law create their own priorities and realities. For example, conflating the risks of transnational organized crime, terrorism, and armed conflict and insurrection to create an exceptionally intrusive and wide-sweeping surveillance, investigatory, and punishment regime of rule of law results in neither further knowledge about organized economic crime nor deterrence respecting civil rights, including privacy. Such an approach tends to make problem solving within any one of these risk areas, which are ultimately grounded in defining and discovering prohibited conduct, more difficult to obtain as the net is spread too far and too wide; this form of organized crime control results in too many false positives, the costs for which are borne both by regulators and wrongfully accused and besmirched persons.

The knowledge and skills required for accurate, complete, and timely calibration of the detection instruments (e.g., global electronic surveillance) to the realities of transnational organized economic crime on the ground, in the neighborhoods, and through cyberspace are inadequately developed and disseminated because the theories and concepts used to explore and explain transnational organized economic crime are materially misleading (e.g., official crime statistics). Policies at the macro (society wide), meso (firm wide), and individual levels (commitment to ethics and integrity) are skewed to protect against inflated international threats (e.g., Islamophobia) at the expense of real domestic threats (e.g., pharmaceuticals such as opioids).

The problem solving suitable for organized crime risk mitigation is different from the risks and circumstances of both international terrorism and domestic insurrection. Putting these three types of wrongful conduct under the same exceptional legal regime distorts the unique challenges to the extant political economy posed by each of these different forms of extralegal conspiracies and acts (Ni Aolain 2019). Understandably, where society leadership (e.g., the U.S. economic elite, politicians) transforms problems within the political economy as wars to be fought, every problem seems to become a target in a war (e.g., the war on terror), notwithstanding (il)logical (in)coherence. Moreover, the threats posed by transnational organized crime gigs may be at a level much lower than the threats posed by transnational organized economic activities that result in offshoring of assets, financial flows, pollution, and so on; that is, the risk of social harm created by the upperworld's dominant but inimical policies and practices dwarf the underworld's threat to the social order.

Experts have opined that traditional organized crime (e.g., NYC's five families) influence can be dramatically mitigated through focused regulation armed with adequate resources; however, questions persist as to whether the old illicit cartels have been displaced by the new licit cartels that trade on stock exchanges with officers and directors garbed in suits, resulting in the up creep of prices and resurgence of deleterious effects on consumers (Morelle 1998, 1233). Traditional organized crime is not the only group presenting the risk of exploitation of consumers and other stakeholders.

The extent to which transnational organized crime presents a red herring and diversion from the real sources and causes of social harm cannot be discerned from deductive and inductive methods of reasoning often deployed in (social) scientific problem solving because the underlying data are inaccurate (e.g., convictions are obtained through compromises of individuals too poor to fight back), incomplete (e.g., detective efforts are inconsistent and made opaque through legally accepted practices such as the exercise of prosecutorial discretion), and reports based thereon are not available timely enough for potential analysts (e.g., investigative journalists, academic scholars) to interpret impartially and independently.

The data required are transactional records, which are generally proprietary, subject to, of course, lawful and unlawful (undisclosed) surveillance by public sector agencies (e.g., the U.S. National Security Agency) and lawful and unlawful custody and use by private sector entities (e.g., financial institutions). Importantly, these records exist. Rare would be an enterprise that did not account for its operations and net (economic) position through income, expense, asset, and liability accounts, albeit not always in conformance with generally accepted accounting principles (GAAP).

The practice of maintaining covert underlying records and consistent failure to file accurate, complete, and timely financial reports to public authorities about the transactions memorialized in these records suggests that transnational organized economic crime may be as much an accounting problem as a law enforcement problem.

Problems such as the risks presented by organized economic crime tend to be described as requiring coordination and collective action among responsible agencies (e.g., organized crime task forces) across different levels (e.g., federal and state law enforcement agencies) for effective and efficient solution, that is, a centralized effort is necessary (Bjelopera and Finkleai 2012b, 38). Theoretically, this problem-solving structure seems appealing; empirically, it seems to work efficaciously with some issues (e.g., soundness and safety of the banking function addressed at the federal level by powerful regulatory agencies such as the Federal Reserve System and the Federal Deposit and Insurance Corporation). However, the operations of organized crime do not result in periodic reports such as those issued by publicly filing corporations to the U.S. Securities and Exchange Commission; nor do organized crime entities have formal compliance functions that would provide an early alert to law enforcement and the public at large.

Organized crime evolves most perniciously and subtly as an underground malignancy, striving to remain an undetectable cancer on the health of society and its legitimate institutions. However, its effects are difficult to measure accurately, at least in a way that would be specifically and forensically auditable and clearly independently and impartially validated. The story of organized crime is recited and disseminated as a historical compilation and analysis, though it is part myth, part truth, and unreliable in material respects. Simply, it is individuals getting together, physically and/or virtually, to engage in wrongful conduct, sometimes illegal, sometimes legal but immoral and unethical, but mostly lacking in transparency. However, at executive levels of influence within the political economy (e.g., high managerial agents), laws may be avoided and financial obligations decreased in creative (yet common in these circles of influence) ways across multiple jurisdictions in significant dollar amounts over numerous periods with comparative impunity (Buettner, Craig, and McIntire 2020). Sometimes, the laws are the problem for those who cannot facilitate workarounds with the appropriate professional services (e.g., lawyers, accountants, bankers, company formation agents, tax havens, and secrecy jurisdictions).

Transnational organized economic crime is a problem sourced in the highest, most prestigious offices of influence in the political economy. It's not just Fat Tony and his goons. It's a way of life that its practitioners at the lower socioeconomic levels deem more worthwhile than working at Mickie D.'s, and it's a way of life that practitioners at higher strata in the socioeconomic structure deem financially way preferable to obeying rules and the spirit of the law. It is amoral.

There are effective means and methods to reduce the risk and harms incident to transnational organized economic crimes. Broadly, these may be conceived as administrative (e.g., mutual agreements and supporting actions among jurisdictions to make such activities unlawful everywhere, reducing the benefits of races to the regulatory bottom), preventive (e.g., having information and communications technologies available and used worldwide, thus expanding the information sharing environment), and detective (e.g., routinizing the programmatic use of forensic auditors in inspection and oversight activities at the cross-border, society wide, and firm wide levels, thus transforming a to date nonroutine *ad hoc* activity into an expected and demanded proactive activity). A mandatorily constructed and imposed, worldwide information sharing environment is necessary. Whether it would be worth the cost (e.g., civil rights, privacy) is unclear.

Specifically, the following evaluative, investigative, and auditing processes could be deployed in more depth and breadth than exists currently:

- Use of artificial intelligence (AI)
- Use of social media
- Use of drones
- Facial recognition technology
- Penetration of the Internet of things (IoT)
- Exploration of cloud services, programs, and files
- Parallel inquiries orchestrated with law enforcement and intelligence agencies

Whether the effects society wide would be desirable remains debatable. Conceivably, a virtual panopticon would transform individuals into beings not altogether different from animals constrained by electronic fences: compliant perhaps; dull indubitably.

Deterring and detecting organized crime demands, among other things, a focused governmental approach, that is, dedicating well-staffed units composed of professionals of diverse skills, including the forensic auditing, consultative evaluating, and independent inspecting of commercial activities—and not a generalized unit whose focus may be too broad (Jacobs and Hortis 1998, 1091). Thus, organized crime control is not a problem to be solved with routine audits; it is not a problem to solved firm-to-firm under a top-down administrative regime overseen by directors and trustees. It is a risk to be mitigated in a manner similar to the object forming the basis of the threat: through collective action utilizing a consortium of specialists (e.g., information security experts and financial analysts) on a worldwide basis.

Moreover, due care should be exercised about the risks presented by organized crime. For example, the problem of organized crime's influence on labor and the ports in New Jersey, United States was recently deemed primarily eradicated (Sherman 2019), notwithstanding the reported difficulty of doing so (Sherman 2018). Risks are inflated and persist over decades (e.g., New York City crime families, Islamic terrorism), and risks are inflated and solved abruptly as noted above. The root and intersection of these risk assessments is the absence of valid and reliable information shared among intelligence agencies, law enforcement agencies, public sector regulators and private sector supervisors, investigative journalists, and most importantly, the public at large.

Ignorance is a vulnerability readily exploitable, especially where the public at large is primed to confirm its own biases. Deceit, half-truths, and myths go a long way, especially where repeated often and saliently in the popular media. Skepticism is not just for auditors.

Just as power is obtained, maintained, and extended in the upper-world via collective action, it is obtained, maintained, and extended in the underworld. Just as hierarchies in the political economy and white markets are transient, reforming, and transforming, hierarchies in the gray and black markets are likewise. The bread-and-butter of the upper- and underworlds are digital currencies transferred at lightning speed across jurisdictions offering cover from disclosure and information and communications technologies that facilitate both the formation of organized actions and the distribution and proceeds. An information sharing environment operated globally under principles and persons of integrity is needed to counter the threat.

References

18 U.S.C. 1951 *et seq.* (as amended 2001). https://law.cornell.edu/uscode/text/18/part-I/chapter-95

Acconcia, A., G. Immordino, S. Piccolo, and P. Rey. 2014. "Accomplice Witnesses and Organized Crime: Theory and Evidence from Italy." *Scandinavian Journal of Economics* 116, no. 4, pp. 1116–59.

Albanese, J.S. 2008. "Risk Assessment in Organized Crime: Developing a Market and Product-Based Model to Determine Threat Levels." *Journal of Contemporary Criminal Justice* 24, no. 3, pp. 263–73.

Albanese, J.S. 2009. "Controlling Organized Crime: Looking for Evidence-Based Approaches." *Victims & Offenders* 4, no. 4, pp. 412–19.

Albanese, J. 2012. "Deciphering the Linkages between Organized Crime and Transnational Crime." *Journal of International Affairs* 66, no. 1, pp. 1XI.

Albanese, J., and P. Reichel. 2014. *Transnational Organized Crime.* Thousand Oaks: SAGE Publications.

Albini, J.L. 1993. "The Mafia and the Devil: What They Have in Common." *Journal of Contemporary Criminal Justice* 9, no. 3, pp. 240–50.

Anglen, R. 2019. "The five families of New York: How the Mafia Divides the City." *Arizona Republic*, March 14, 2019. https://azcentral.com/story/news/local/arizona-investigations/2017/10/31/five-families-new-york-how-mafia-divides-city/777899001/

Arsovska, J. 2008. "Interviewing Serious Offenders: Ms. Egghead Meets Mr. Gumshoe." *Trends in Organized Crime* 11, no. 1, pp. 42–58.

Asmann, P., S. Dudley, and C. Molinares. 2020. "The Professor and the Fixer: How a Colombian Middleman Got a Crime Specialist to Launder Money." *InSight Crime*, June 25, 2020. https://insightcrime.org/news/analysis/professor-fixer-colombia-middleman-crime-specialist-launder-money/

Barron, J. 2014. "Details of Sharpton's Time as Informer Shed Light on a Life with Many Chapters." *New York Times*, April 8, 2014. https://nytimes.com/2014/04/09/nyregion/details-of-sharptons-time-as-informer-shed-light-on-a-life-with-many-chapters.html?searchResultPosition=2

Baud, C. n.d. "1970: 'Entirely too Comfortable' with the Jersey Mafia." *Trentonian*, n.d. http://capitalcentury.com/1970.html

Beare, M.E. 2007. "The Devil Made Me Do It: Business Partners in Crime." *Journal of Financial Crime* 14, no. 1, pp. 34–48.

Berry, L.B., G.E. Curtis, S.L. Elan, R.A. Hudson, and N.A. Kollars. 2003. "Transnational Activities of Chinese Crime Organizations." *Library of*

Congress, April 2003. https://globalsecurity.org/military/library/report/2003/chinese-org-crime.pdf

Bjelopera, J.P., and K.M. Finklea. 2012a. "Organized Crime: An Evolving Challenge for U.S. Law Enforcement." *Congressional Research Service,* January 6, 2012. https://fas.org/sgp/crs/misc/R41547.pdf

Bjelopera, J.P., and K.M. Finklea. 2012b. "Organized Crime: An Evolving Challenge for U.S. Law Enforcement." *Congressional Research Service,* January 6, 2012. https://fas.org/sgp/crs/misc/R41547.pdf

Blakey, G.R. 1990. "Symposium Law and the Continuing Enterprise: Perspectives on RICO: Foreword." *Notre Dame Law Review* 65, pp. 873–1106.

Brown, R. 2009. "The Tri-Border Area: A Profile of the Largest Illicit Economy in the Western Hemisphere." *Financial Transparency Coalition,* June 15, 2009. https://financialtransparency.org/the-tri-border-area-a-profile-of-the-largest-illicit-economy-in-the-western-hemisphere/

Bruns, M. 2015. "A Network Approach to Organized Crime by the Dutch Public Sector." *Police Practice and Research* 16, no. 2, pp. 161–74.

Buettner, R., S. Craig, and M. McIntire. 2020. "The President's Taxes." *New York Times,* September 28, 2020. https://nytimes.com/interactive/2020/09/27/us/donald-trump-taxes.html

Byron, C. 1990. "The Bottom Line: Bad Music." *New York* 23, no. 30, p. 10.

Calderoni, F. 2015. "The Analysis and Containment of Organized Crime and Transnational Organized Crime: An Interview with Ernesto U. Savona." *Trends in Organized Crime* 18, nos. (1/2), 128–42. doi:10.1007/s12117-014-9232-x

Cara, A. October 2015. "Modus Operandi off Organized Crime. Violence, Corruption, and Money Laundering." *European Scientific Journal* 11, no. 28.

Carrapico, H., D. Irrera, and B. Tupman. 2014. "Transnational Organised Crime and Terrorism: Different Peas, Same Pod?" *Global Crime* 15, nos. 3–4, 213–18. doi: 10.1080/17440572.2014.939882

Carroll, L. (aka Charles L. Dodgson). 1872. *Through the Looking-Glass.* Chapter 6, p. 205 (1934). First published in 1872.

Center for the Study of Democracy. 2010. "Examining the Links Between Organized Crime and Corruption." https://ec.europa.eu/home-affairs/sites/homeaffairs/files/doc_centre/crime/docs/study_on_links_between_organised_crime_and_corruption_en.pdf

Central Intelligence Agency. 2008. "Testimony on International Organized Crime." https://cia.gov/news-information/speeches-testimony/1996/carey_13196.html

Chapman, B. 2020. "High Street Banks Guilty of 'Serious Organised Crime' Against Customers, Says Police Commissioner." *Independent,* June 4, 2020. https://independent.co.uk/news/business/news/uk-banks-signature-forgery-police-commissioner-crime-nca-a9547941.html

Chepesiuk, R. (blog). 2011. "The Myths of Organized Crime." *Maverick House*, July 11, 2011. https://maverickhouse.blogspot.com/2011/07/myths-of-organized-crime.html

Choi, C.Q. 2014. "What a Perfect Heist Can Teach you about National Security." *Popular Mechanics*, August 22, 2014. https://popularmechanics.com/military/a11132/what-a-perfect-heist-can-teach-you-about-national-security-17123172/

Citizens United v. Federal Election Commission. 2010. 558 U.S. 301, https://law.cornell.edu/supct/pdf/08-205P.ZS

Clancy, N. 2019. "Mexico City Sounds Alarm on Potential Transformation of its Gangs." *InSight Crime*, March 29, 2019. https://insightcrime.org/news/brief/officials-sound-alarm-transformation-mexico-city-gangs/

Cockburn, A. 2020. "The Malaysian Job." *Harper's Magazine*, May 2020. https://harpers.org/archive/2020/05/the-malaysian-job-wolf-of-wall-street-1malaysia-development-berhad/

Cooper, S. 2019. "'Organized Crime Knows Fraud is the way to go': Former RCMP Financial Crime Expert." *Global News*, July 8, 2019. https://globalnews.ca/news/5463766/organized-crime-knows-fraud-is-the-way-to-go-former-rcmp-financial-crime-expert/

Council of Europe. 2015. "Typologies Report on Laundering the Proceeds of Organized Crime." *MONEYVAL*, April 17, 2015. https://rm.coe.int/typologies-report-on-laundering-the-proceeds-of-organised-crime/168071509d

Council on Foreign Relations. 2013. "The Global Regime for Transnational Organized Crime." *International Institutions and Governance Program*, June 25, 2013. https://cfr.org/report/global-regime-transnational-crime

Cox, J. 2020. "How Police Secretly Took Over a Global Phone Network for Organized Crime." *VICE*, July 2, 2020. https://vice.com/en_us/article/3aza95/how-police-took-over-encrochat-hacked

Cressey, D.R. 1969. "Theft of the Nation." *Harper's Magazine*, February 1969.

Critchley, D. 2009. *The Origin of Organized Crime in America the New York City Mafia, 1891–1931*. New York, NY: Routledge.

Croall, H. 2010. "Phantom Fraudsters Still: Re-Viewing Long-Firm Fraud." *Global Crime* 11, no. 3, pp. 340–45. doi: 10.1080/17440572.2010.490641

DelBosque, M. 2017. *Blood Lines the True Story of a Drug Cartel, the FBI, and the Battle for a Horse-Racing Dynasty*. New York, NY: HarperCollins Publishers.

Del Monte, D., G. Riva, and S. Vergine. 2020. "Murder, Drugs, and Extortion in Tuscany's Chinese Underworld." *Organized Crime and Corruption Reporting Project*, July 30, 2020. https://occrp.org/en/investigations/murder-drugs-and-extortion-in-tuscanys-chinese-underworld

Dimico, A., A. Isopi, and O. Olsson. 2017. "Origins of the Sicilian Mafia: The Market for Lemons." *The Journal of Economic History* 77, no. 4, pp. 1083–1115. doi:10.1017/S002205071700078X

Diittmar, V. 2020. "Why the Jalisco Cartel does not Dominate Mexico's Criminal Landscape." *InSight Crime,* June 11, 2020. https://insightcrime.org/news/analysis/jalisco-cartel-dominate-mexico/

Douven, I. 2017. "Abduction." In *The Stanford Encyclopedia of Philosophy* (Summer 2017 edition), ed. E.N. Zalta., https://plato.stanford.edu/archives/sum2017/entries/abduction/

Drew, J. 2015. "CPAs: Criminal Pursuing Agents." *Journal of Accountancy,* October 1, 2015. https://journalofaccountancy.com/issues/2015/oct/cpa-criminal-investigators.html

Dudley, S. 2016. "Elites and organized crime: Conceptual Framework – Organized Crime." *InSight Crime,* March 23, 2016. https://insightcrime.org/investigations/elites-and-organized-crime-conceptual-framework-organized-crime/

Edwards, A., and P. Gill. 2002. "Crime as Enterprise? The Case of 'transnational Organised Crime'." *Crime, Law and Social Change* 37, no. 3, pp. 203–223.

Emerging technology from the arXiv. 2014. "Economic Network of Organized Crime Revealed." *MIT Technology Review,* March 25, 2014. https://technologyreview.com/s/525826/economic-network-of-organized-crime-revealed/

Europol. 2018. "Crime on the Dark Web: Law Enforcement Coordination is the Only Cure." *Europol Press Release,* May 29, 2018. https://europol.europa.eu/newsroom/news/crime-dark-web-law-enforcement-coordination-only-cure.

Europol. 2020. "Enterprising criminals - Europe's Fight Against the Global Networks of Financial and Economic Crime." *European Union Agency for Law Enforcement Cooperation,* June 5, 2020. https://europol.europa.eu/publications-documents/enterprising-criminals-%E2%80%93-europe%E2%80%99s-fight-against-global-networks-of-financial-and-economic-crime

Evans, D.M. 1859. *Facts, Failures, and Frauds: Revelations, Financial, Mercantile, Criminal.* London: Groombridge and Sons.

FBI. 2005. "Final Accounting Numbers Add up to Mob Boss's Conviction." https://archives.fbi.gov/archives/news/stories/2005/november/massino_110205

FBI. n.d. "Transnational Organized Crime." https://fbi.gov/investigate/organized-crime

FBI News. 2018. "International Criminal Communications Service Dismantled." *FBI News,* March 16, 2018. https://fbi.gov/news/stories/phantom-secure-takedown-031618

Finckenauer, J.O. 2007. "La Cosa Nostra in the United States." https://ncjrs.gov/pdffiles1/nij/218555.pdf

Finckenauer, J.O., and K.L. Chin. 2004. "Asian Transnational Organized Crime and Its Impact on the United States: Developing a Transnational Crime Research Agenda." https://ncjrs.gov/pdffiles1/nij/grants/213310.pdf

Finklea, K.M. 2010. "Organized crime in the United States: Trends and issues for Congress." *Congressional Research Service,* December 22, 2010. https://fas.org/sgp/crs/misc/R40525.pdf

Fisher, S., and Q.E. Lab. 2020. "A Fractured System: Mexico's Criminal Investigation Network." *InSight Crime*, July 1, 2020. https://insightcrime.org/news/analysis/a-fractured-system-mexico/

Fitzgibbon, W. 2020. "Unchecked by Global Banks, Dirty Cash Destroys Dreams and Lives." *International Consortium of Investigative Journalists*, September 20, 2020. https://icij.org/investigations/fincen-files/unchecked-by-global-banks-dirty-cash-destroys-dreams-and-lives/?utm_source=ICIJ&utm_campaign=acfdcff1d4-0920_WeeklyEmail&utm_medium=email&utm_term=0_992ecfdbb2-acfdcff1d4-82296497

Fitzgibbon, W, and B. Hallman. 2020. "What is a Tax Haven? Offshore Finance, Explained." *International Consortium of Investigative Journalists*, April 6, 2020. https://icij.org/investigations/panama-papers/what-is-a-tax-haven-offshore-finance-explained/

Foster, M.A. 2019. "Bribery, Kickbacks, and Self-Dealing: An Overview of Honest Services Fraud and Issues for Congress." *Congressional Research Service*, January 30, 2019. https://fas.org/sgp/crs/misc/R45479.pdf

Fricke, D. 1992. "Jimi: The Man and the Music." *Rolling Stone*, no. 623, p. 40.

Georgetown Security Studies Review. 2018. "Bitcoin and the Dark Web: The New Terrorist Threat?" https://georgetownsecuritystudiesreview.org/2018/01/21/bitcoin-and-the-dark-web-the-new-terrorist-threat/

Glebovskiy, A. 2019. "Inherent Criminogenesis in Business Organisations." *Journal of Financial Crime* 26, no. 2, pp. 432–46.

Gold, M. 2019. "Gambino Crime Family: How Control has Changed Since the 1950s." *New York Times*, March 14, 2019. https://nytimes.com/2019/03/14/nyregion/gambino-crime-family.html

Guccione, D. 2020. "What is the dark web? How to access it and what you'll find." *CSO*, March 5, 2020. https://csoonline.com/article/3249765/what-is-the-dark-web-how-to-access-it-and-what-youll-find.html

Henning, P.J. 2018. "RICO Lawsuits are Tempting, But Tread Lightly." *New York Times*, January 16, 2018. https://nyti.ms/2FL1zvY

History. 2019. "The Demise of the Mafia." https://history.com/topics/crime/the-demise-of-the-mafia

Hobbs, D. 2012. "'It Was Never About The Money' Market Society, Organized Crime, and UK Criminology." In *New Directions in Criminological Theory*, pp. 257–75. London: Routledge.

Hobbs, D., and C. Dunnighan. 1998. "Glocal Organised Crime: Context and Pretext." In *The New European Criminology: Crime and Social Order in Europe*, ed. V. Ruggiero, N. South, and I. Taylor, pp. 289–303. London, England: Routledge.

Hobbs, D., and G.A. Antonopoulos. 2013. "Endemic to the Species': Ordering the 'other' via Organised Crime." *Global Crime* 14, no. 1, pp. 27–51.

Holden, ed. n.d. "An Introduction to Tor vs 12P." *IVPN Privacy Guides*. https://ivpn.net/privacy-guides/an-introduction-to-tor-vs-i2p

Holden, S. 1990. "Book of the Times; High Price of Putting a Song in the Heart." *New York Times*, August 27, 1990. https://nytimes.com/1990/08/27/books/books-of-the-times-high-price-of-putting-a-song-in-the-heart.html?searchResultPosition=2

Holland, B. 2019. "How the Mob Helped Establish NYC's Gay Bar Scene." https://history.com/news/how-the-mob-helped-establish-nycs-gay-bar-scene.

Holloway, L. 2002. "Media: Arrests Illustrate a Growing Concern Over Bootlegged Recordings." *New York Times*, December 2, 2002. https://nytimes.com/2002/12/02/business/media-arrests-illustrate-a-growing-concern-over-bootlegged-recordings.html?searchResultPosition=1

Hortis, C.A., and J.B. Jacobs. 2014. *The Mob and the City the Hidden History of How the Mafia Captured New York*. Amherst, NY: Prometheus Books.

InSight Crime. 2019. "Elites and Organized Crime." *InSight Crime*, October 25, 2019. https://insightcrime.org/indepth/elites-and-organized-crime/

INTERPOL. 2020. "INTERPOL Hosts Police Chiefs Meeting to Combat 'Ndrangheta." *INTERPOL*, June 24, 2020. https://interpol.int/en/News-and-Events/News/2020/INTERPOL-hosts-police-chiefs-meeting-to-combat-Ndrangheta

Jacobs, J.B., and A.Hortis. 1998. "New York City as Organized Crime Fighter." *New York Law School Law Review* 42, pp. 1069–1255.

Jacobs, J.B., and L.P. Gouldin. 1999. "Cosa Nostra: The Final Chapter?" *Crime and Justice* 25, pp. 129–291.

Jacobs, J.B., and R.P. Alford. 2005. "The Teamsters Rocky Road to Recovery—The Demise of Project Rise." *Trends in Organized Crime* 9, no. 1, pp. 5–23. doi:10.1007/s12117-005-1001-4

Jacobs, J.B., and Project Muse. 2006. *Mobsters, Unions, and Feds: The Mafia and the American Labor Movement*. UPCC Book Collections on Project MUSE. New York: New York University Press.

James, M. 2012. "The Other Civil Society: Organised Crime in Fragile and Failing States." *Defence Studies* 12, no. 2, pp. 218–56.

Jaspers, J.D. 2019. "Business Cartels and Organised Crime: Exclusive and Inclusive Systems of Collusion." *Trends in Organized Crime* 22, no. 4, pp. 414–32. doi:10.1007/s12117-018-9350-y

Johnson, M. 2020a. "Italian Mafia Bonds Sold to Global Investors." *Financial Times*, July 7, 2020. https://ft.com/content/bcebd77c-057b-4fd0-bd99-b97e0e559455

Johnson, M. 2020b. "How the Mafia Infiltrated Italy's Hospitals and Laundered the Profits Globally." *Financial Times*, July 9, 2020. https://amp.ft.com/content/8850581c-176e-4c5c-8b38-debb26b35c14

Justice Information Sharing. 2013. "Title III of the Omnibus Crime Control and Safe Streets Act of 1968." https://it.ojp.gov/PrivacyLiberty/authorities/statutes/1284

Karstedt, S., M. Levi, and B. Godfrey. 2006. "Markets, Risk and 'White-collar' Crimes: Moral Economies from Victorian times to Enron." *British Journal of Criminology* 46, no. 6, pp. 971–75.

Klima, N., N. Dorn, and T.V. Beken. 2011. "Risk Calculation and Precautionary Uncertainty: Two Configurations within Crime Assessment." *Crime, Law and Social Change* 55, no. 1, pp. 15–31.

Koehler, M. 2020. "AG Barr's Recent Speech is FCPA Relevant." *FCPA* (foreign corrupt practices act) blog. September 21, 2020. https://fcpaprofessor.com/ag-barrs-recent-speech-fcpa-relevant/#more-29712

Koivu, K.L. 2018. "Illicit Partners and Political Development: How Organized Crime Made the State." *Studies in Comparative International Development* 53, no. 1, pp. 47–66.

Lafleur, J.M., L.K. Purvis, and A.W. Roesler. 2015. "The Perfect Heist: Recipes from Around the World." *Sandia National Laboratories*, March 2015. https://prod-ng.sandia.gov/techlib-noauth/access-control.cgi/2014/141790.pdf

Lars, K., and P. Larsson. 2011. "Organized Crime the Nordic Way." *Crime and Justice* 40, no. 1, pp. 519–54.

Lavorgna, A., and A. Sergi. 2016. "Serious, Therefore Organised? A Critique of the Emerging "Cyber-Organised Crime" Rhetoric in the United Kingdom." *International Journal of Cyber Criminology* 10, no. 2, pp. 170–87.

Lawfare (blog). 2019. "Transnational Organized Crime and National Security." https://lawfareblog.com/transnational-organized-crime-and-national-security-0

Lesieur, H.R. 1979. "Book Review: Illegal But Not Criminal: Business Crime in America, Corporate and Governmental Deviance: Problems of Organizational Behavior in Contemporary Society, White-Collar Crime: Offenses in Business, Politics and the Professions, Crimes of the Powerful: Marxism, Crime and Deviance, Crime at the Top: Deviance in Business and the Professions, Official Deviance: Readings in Malfeasance, Misfeasance and Other Forms of Corruption." *Criminal Justice Review* 4, no. 1, pp. 95–100.

Leukfeldt, E., A. Lavorgna, and E. Kleemans. 2017. "Organised Cybercrime or Cybercrime That Is Organised? An Assessment of the Conceptualisation of Financial Cybercrime as Organised Crime." *European Journal on Criminal Policy and Research* 23, no. 3, pp. 287–300.

Levi, M. 2008. "Organized Fraud and Organizing Frauds: Unpacking Research on Networks and Organization." *Criminology & Criminal Justice* 8, no. 4, pp. 389–419.

Levi, M. 2010. "The Phantom Capitalists Ride Again: A Response to My Critics." *Global Crime* 11, no. 3, pp. 350–54.

Levi, M. 2012. "States, Frauds, and the Threat of Transnational Organized Crime." *Journal of International Affairs* 66, no. 1, 39XIV. https://ez.lib. jjay.cuny.edu/login?url=https://search-proquest-com.ez.lib.jjay.cuny.edu/ docview/1243042446?accountid=11724

Levi, M. 2016. "The Impacts of Organised Crime in the EU: Some Preliminary Thoughts on Measurement Difficulties." *Contemporary Social Science: Crime and Society* 11, no. 4, pp. 392–402.

Levin, B. 2013. "American Gangsters: RICO, Criminal Syndicates, and Conspiracy Law as Market Control." *Harvard Civil Rights - Civil Liberties Law Review* 48, no. 1, pp. 105ff-105ff.

Lichtenstein, G. 1974. "CBS News Tells of Payola on Records." *New York Times*, August 10, 1974. https://nytimes.com/1974/08/10/archives/cbs-news-tells-of-payola-on-records.html?searchResultPosition=3

Liddick, D. 1999. "The Enterprise "Model" of Organized Crime: Assessing Theoretical Propositions." *Justice Quarterly* 16, no. 2, pp. 403–30.

Lloyd, A. 2020. "Working for Free Illegal Employment Practices, 'off the Books' Work and the Continuum of Legality within the Service Economy." *Trends in Organized Crime* 23, no. 1, pp. 77–93. doi:10.1007/s12117-018-9351-x

Lloyd, T. 2020. "FBI concerned over laundering risks in private equity, hedge funds – leaked document." *Reuters*, July 14, 2020. https://reuters.com/article/ bc-finreg-fbi-laundering-private-equity-idUSKCN24F1TP.

Lombardi, E. 2019. "Upton Sinclair Quotes." *ThoughtCo.*, March 2, 2019. https://thoughtco.com/upton-sinclair-quotes-741426.

Lombardo, R.M. 2013a. "Explaining Organized Crime." In *Organized Crime in Chicago: Beyond the Mafia*, 15–36. University of Illinois Press. www.jstor.org/ stable/10.5406/j.ctt2tt9mc.5

Lombardo, R.M. 2013b. "Fighting Organized Crime: A History of Law Enforcement Efforts in Chicago." *Journal of Contemporary Criminal Justice* 29, no. 2, pp. 296–316.

Lord, N.J, L.J Campbell, and K.V. Wingerde. 2019. "Other People's Dirty Money: Professional Intermediaries, Market Dynamics and the Finances of White-Collar, Corporate and Organized Crimes." *British Journal of Criminology* 59, no. 5, pp. 1217–36.

Lurigio, A.J, and J.J. Binder. 2013. "The Chicago Outfit: Challenging the Myths About Organized Crime." *Journal of Contemporary Criminal Justice* 29, no. 2, pp. 198–218.

Marker, M.D. 2019. "Organized Crime has Gone High Tech." *International Association of Chiefs of Police (IACP)*, http://policechiefmagazine.org/organized-crime-has-gone-high-tech/?ref=84d61b015afa1c81706a083d70913b6c

Marshall, Jonathan. 2018. "The dictator and the mafia: How Rafael Trujillo partnered with US criminals to extend his power." *Journal of Global South Studies* 35, no. 1, pp. 56–86.

Matsangou, E. 2017. "Organized Crime: The Economic Underbelly." *World Finance*, January 16, 2017. https://worldfinance.com/wealth-management/organised-crime-the-economic-underbelly

Maurer, D.W. 1940. *The Big Con: The Story of the Confidence Man*. New York, NY: Anchor Books.

McCarthy, E. 2019. "Article: A Call to Prosecute Drug Company Fraud as Organized Crime." *Syracuse Law Review* 69, pp. 439–502.

McCusker, R. 2006. "Transnational Organised Cyber Crime: Distinguishing Threat from Reality." *Crime, Law and Social Change* 46, no. 4–5, pp. 257–73.

McIllwain, J. 2015. "On the History, Theory, and Practice of Organized Crime: The Life and Work of Criminology's Revisionist 'Godfather,' Joseph L. Albini (1930–2013)." *Trends in Organized Crime* 18, nos. (1/2), pp. 12–40. doi:10.1007/s12117-014-9236-6

Middleton, D., and M. Levi. 2015. "Let Sleeping Lawyers Lie: Organized Crime, Lawyers and the Regulation of Legal Services." *British Journal Of Criminology* 55, no. 4, pp. 647–68.

Migration Policy Institute. 2018. "Transnational Organized Crime Groups, Immigration and Border Security: Connections, Distinctions, and Proposals for Effective Policy." https://migrationpolicy.org/research/transnational-organized-crime-groups-immigration-border-security

Milhaupt, C., and M. West. 2000. "The Dark Side of Private Ordering: An Institutional and Empirical Analysis of Organized Crime." *The University of Chicago Law Review* 67, no. 1, pp. 41–98.

Mills, H., S. Skodbo, and P. Blyth. 2013. "Understanding Organised Crime: Estimating the Scale and Social and Economic Costs." *Research Report* 73, *Home Office (U.K.)*, October 2013. https://assets.publishing.service.gov.uk/government/uploads/system/uploads/attachment_data/file/246390/horr73.pdf

Mirenda, L., S. Mocetti, and L. Rizzica. 2019. "The Boss on Board: Mafia Infiltration, Firm Performance, and Local Economic Growth." *VOX*, October 26, 2019. https://voxeu.org/article/mafia-infiltrations-firm-performance-and-local-economic-growth

Mob Museum. n.d. "Prohibition Profits Transformed the Mob." http://prohibition.themobmuseum.org/the-history/the-rise-of-organized-crime/the-mob-during-prohibition/

Monterrosa-Yancey, K. 2017. "Forensic Accounting in the Fight Against Financial Crimes." *ACAMSTODAY*, May 23, 2017. https://acamstoday.org/forensic-accounting-fight-against-financial-crimes/

Morrison, S. 2020. "All Eyes Turn to Apple as Antitrust Investigations Heat Up." *Vox*, June 16, 2020. https://vox.com/recode/2020/6/16/21292973/apple-antitrust-european-union-commission-spotify

Moynihan, C. 2019. "The Yoga Instructors vs the Private Equity Firm." *New York Times*, September 12, 2019. https://nytimes.com/2019/09/11/nyregion/yoga-instructor-union.html

Morelle, M.E. 1998. "'Something Smells Fishy': The Giuliani Administration's Effort to Rid the Commercial Trade Waste Collection Industry of Organized Crime." *New York Law School Law Review* 42, nos. 3 & 4, pp. 1213–38.

Naím, M. 2012. "Mafia States: Organized Crime Takes Office." *Foreign Affairs* 91, no. 3: pp. 100–111.

Nakamura, K., G. Tita, and D. Krackhardt. 2020. "Violence in the 'Balance': A Structural Analysis of How Rivals, Allies, and Third-Parties Shape Inter-Gang Violence." *Global Crime*, 21, no. 1, pp. 3–27, doi: 10.1080/17440572.2019.1627879

Napoliello, A. 2020. "Pagans Biker Gang is a Growing Threat to the Public in N.J. Here's How Officials Believe it can be Stopped." *NJ Advance Media*, September 9, 2020. https://nj.com/crime/2020/09/pagans-biker-gang-is-a-growing-threat-to-the-public-in-nj-heres-how-officials-believe-it-can-be-stopped.html

National Conference of State Legislatures. 2017. "Independent Expenditures." *NCSL*, July 21, 2017. https://ncsl.org/research/elections-and-campaigns/independent-expenditures635425050.aspx

National Crime Agency. 2019. "National Strategic Assessment of Serious and Organized Crime." https://nationalcrimeagency.gov.uk/who-we-are/publications/296-national-strategic-assessment-of-serious-organised-crime-2019/file

National Security Council. 2011. "Transnational Organized Crime: A Growing Threat to National and International Security." https://obamawhitehouse.archives.gov/administration/eop/nsc/transnational-crime/threat

Ni Aolain, F. 2019. "A Post-Mortem on UN Security Council Resolution 2482 on Organized Crime and Counter-Terrorism." *Just Security*, August 12, 2019. https://justsecurity.org/65777/a-post-mortem-on-un-security-council-resolution-2482-on-organized-crime-and-counter-terrorism/

Nicola, A.D, and A. Scartezzini. 2000. "When Economic Crime Becomes Organised: The Role of Information Technologies. A Case Study." *Current Issues in Criminal Justice* 11, no. 3, pp. 343–48.

O'Brien, R.D. 2019. "Investment Bankers Charged in Global Insider-Trading Scheme." *Wall Street Journal*, October 22, 2019. https://wsj.com/articles/investment-bankers-charged-in-global-insider-trading-scheme-11571763384?shareToken=st24bd90e3991f4ec99c59a3ae48390e31

Office of the Director of National Intelligence. 2018. "Worldwide Threat Assessment of the U.S. Intelligence Community." https://dni.gov/files/documents/Newsroom/Testimonies/2018-ATA—Unclassified-SSCI.pdf

Office of the Director of National Intelligence. 2020. "Five Eyes Intelligence Oversight and Review Council." https://dni.gov/index.php/who-we-are/ organizations/enterprise-capacity/chco/chco-related-menus/chco-related-links/recruitment-and-outreach/217-about/organization/icig-pages/2660-icig-fiorc

Ogle, V. 2020. "'Funk Money': The End of Empires, The Expansion of Tax Havens, and Decolonization as an Economic and Financial Event." *Past & Present (online)*, August 23, 2020. https://doi.org/10.1093/pastj/gtaa001

Oliver, M. 2019. "Inside the Yakuza, The 400-Hundred-Year-Old Japanese Criminal Syndicate." *ati*, April 30, 2019. https://allthatsinteresting.com/ yakuza-history

Ott, T.P. 2010. "US Law Enforcement Strategies to Combat Organized Crime Threats to Financial Institutions." *Journal of Financial Crime* 17, no. 4, 375–86. doi:10.1108/13590791011082742. www.scopus.com

Papadovassilakis, A. 2020. "Guatemala Imposes Martial Law Under Pretext of Combating Organized Crime." *InSight Crime*, July 27, 2020. https:// insightcrime.org/news/analysis/martial-law-guatemala-crime/

Perri, F.S., and R.G. Brody. 2011. "The Dark Triad: Organized Crime, Terror and Fraud." *Journal of Money Laundering Control* 14, no. 1, pp. 44–59.

Pistor, K. 2020. "The Debt Predators." *Project Syndicate*, July 20, 2020. https:// project-syndicate.org/commentary/debt-predators-ruin-households-firms-governments-by-katharina-pistor-2020-07

Police Foundation and Perpetuity Research. 2017. "The Impact of Organized Crime in Local Communities." https://perpetuityresearch.com/wp-content/ uploads/2017/06/2017-05-Organised-Crime-in-Local-Communities-Final-Report-web.pdf

Quan, D. 2019. "Exclusive: RCMP's New Strategy for Tackling Terrorism, Organized Crime – Accountants, Computer Whizzes and Data Geeks." *National Post*, April 23, 2019. https://nationalpost.com/news/canada/ exclusive-rcmps-new-strategy-for-tackling-terrorism-organized-crime-accountants-computer-whizzes-and-data-geeks

Quintero, T.L. 2017. "The Connected Black Market: How the Dark Web has Empowered LatAm Organized Crime." *InSight Crime*, September 13, 2017. https://insightcrime.org/news/analysis/connected-black-market-how-dark-web-empowered-latam-organized-crime/

Raab, S. 1984. "Ex-crime Figure is Expected to Testify on Laundering of Billions in Banks." *New York Times*, March 13, 1984. https://nytimes.com/1984/03/13/ nyregion/ex-crime-figure-is-expected-to-testify-on-laundering-of-billions-in-banks.html?searchResultPosition=9

Raab, S. 2005. *Five Families: The Rise, Decline, and Resurgence of America's Most Powerful Mafia Empires*. New York, NY: St. Martin's Press.

Raab, S. 2019. "Carmine Persico, Colombo Crime Family Boss, is Dead at 85." *New York Times*, March 8, 2019. https://nytimes.com/2019/03/08/obituaries/carmine-j-persico-colombo-crime-family-boss-is-dead-at-85.html?searchResultPosition=5

Ravenda, D., M.M Valencia-Silva, J.M. Argiles-Bosch, and J. Garcia-Blandon. 2018. "Accrual Management as an Indication of Money Laundering through Legally Registered Mafia Firms in Italy." *Accounting, Auditing & Accountability Journal* 31, no. 1, pp. 286–317.

Reynolds, L., and M. McKee. 2010. "Organised Crime and the Efforts to Combat It: A Concern for Public Health.(Review)." *Globalization and Health* 6, no. 21. http://dx.doi.org.ez.lib.jjay.cuny.edu/10.1186/1744-8603-6-21

Rosenblum, M.R., J.P. Bjelopera, and K.M. Finklea. 2013. "Border Security: Understanding Threats at U.S. Borders." *Congressional Research Service, February 21, 2013*. https://fas.org/sgp/crs/homesec/R42969.pdf

Ross, E. 2007. "Sin and Society." *Multinational Monitor*, 28, no. 3, pp. 41–45.

Rowe, E., T. Akman, R.G. Smith, and A. Tomison. 2013. "Organized Crime and Public Sector Corruption: A Crime Scripts Analysis of Tactical Displacement Risks." *Australian Institute of Criminology*, no. 444, pp. 1–7. https://aic.gov.au/publications/tandi/tandi444

Ruggiero, V. 2019. "Hypotheses on the Causes of Financial Crime." *Journal of Financial Crime* 27, no. 1, pp. 245–57.

Russo, G. 2001. *The Outfit: The Role of Chicago's Underworld in the Shaping of Modern America*, 1st U.S. ed., New York, NY: Bloomsbury: Distributed to the Trade by Holtzbrinck Publishers.

Russo, G. 2006. *Supermob : How Sidney Korshak and His Criminal Associates Became America's Hidden Power Brokers*, 1st U.S. ed., New York, NY: Bloomsbury: Distributed to the Trade by Holtzbrinck.

Salomon, J., H.S. Avalos, and P. Asmann. 2020. "State Intelligence and Organized Crime: An Old Relationship in Latin America." *Insight Crime*, June 19, 2020. https://insightcrime.org/news/analysis/state-intelligence-crime-latin-america//

Schenck, J. 2017. "Emerging Financial Crime Threats for 2018." *ACAMSTODAY*, December 12, 2017. https://acamstoday.org/emerging-financial-crime-threats-for-2018/

Schladebeck, J. 2016. "A Look at the Gambino Crime Family Tree, from their Early Roots to Serving as Inspiration for 'The Godfather'." *Daily News*, August 24, 2016. https://nydailynews.com/news/national/gambino-crime-family-tree-article-1.2764033

Security Intelligence. 2016. "Dark Web Suppliers and Organized Cybercrime Gigs." https://securityintelligence.com/dark-web-suppliers-and-organized-cybercrime-gigs/

Sergi, A. 2015. "Organised Crime in English Criminal Law." *Journal of Money Laundering Control* 18, no. 2, pp. 182–201.

Sergi, A. 2018. "What's Really Going on in London's Organized Crime Scene – According to a Criminologist." https://theconversation.com/whats-really-going-on-in-londons-organised-crime-scene-according-to-a-criminologist-88659

Sergi, A. 2020. "Mafia Organizations: The Visible Hand of Criminal Enterprise by Maurizio Catino." *Trends in Organized Crime* 23, no. 2, pp. 183–85. *Gale Academic OneFile,* https://link-gale-com.ez.lib.jjay.cuny.edu/apps/doc/A625363938/AONE?u=cuny_johnjay&sid=AONE&xid=d27a43cc (accessed on August 7, 2020).

Sergi, A., and L. Storti. 2020. "Survive or Perish: Organised Crime in the Port of Montreal and the Port of New York/New Jersey." *International Journal of Law, Crime and Justice,* August 2, 2020 (online), https://doi.org/10.1016/j.ijlcj.2020.100424

Shaw, D. 2020. "Hundreds Arrested as Crime Chat Network Cracked." *BBC News,* July 2, 2020. https://bbc.com/news/uk-53263310

Sherman, T. 2019. "We Don't Need a Watchdog Agency to Police the Mob on the Waterfront, State Says." *NJ Advance Media,* September 18, 2019. https://nj.com/politics/2019/09/we-dont-need-a-watchdog-agency-to-police-the-mob-on-the-waterfront-state-says.html

Sherman, T. 2018. "'Guys Like that Don't Get Wiped Out in a Day.' Why the Mob Still Holds Sway at the Port." *NJ Advance Media,* July 2018. https://nj.com/news/2018/07/at_jerseys_ports_the_shadow_of_the_mob_never_goes.html

Silverstone, D. 2011. "A Response To: Morselli, C., Turcotte, M. and Tenti, V. 2010. The Mobility of Criminal Groups." *Global Crime: Spatial Mobility and Organised Crime* 12, no. 3, pp. 189–206.

Skilling v. United States 2010. 561 U.S. 358, 2010. https://law.cornell.edu/supct/pdf/08-1394P.ZO

Sproat, P. 2012. "Phoney War or Appeasement? The Policing of Organised Crime in the UK." *Trends in Organized Crime* 15, no. 4, pp. 313–30.

Sterling, T. 2019. "Google to end 'Double Irish, Dutch Sandwich' Tax Scheme." *Reuters,* December 31, 2019. https://reuters.com/article/us-google-taxes-netherlands-idUSKBN1YZ10Z

Stout, L. 2010. "How Hedge Funds Create Criminals." *Harvard Business Review,* December 13, 2010. https://hbr.org/2010/12/how-hedge-funds-create-crimina

Sucher, J. 2014. "Music and the Mob." https://huffpost.com/entry/music-and-the-mob_b_5509816

Szczepanski, K. 2019. "History of Japanese Organized Crime, the Yakuza." *ThoughtCo,* July 17, 2019. https://thoughtco.com/the-yakuza-organized-crime-195571

Taibbi, M. 2012. "The Scam Wall Street Learned from the Mafia." *Rolling Stone*, June 21, 2012. https://rollingstone.com/politics/politics-news/the-scam-wall-street-learned-from-the-mafia-190232/

Tax Justice Network. 2020. "Watershed Data Indicates more than a Trillion Dollars of Corporate Profit Smuggled into Tax Havens." *Tax Justice Network*, July 8, 2020. https://taxjustice.net/2020/07/08/watershed-data-indicates-more-than-a-trillion-dollars-of-corporate-profit-smuggled-into-tax-havens/?utm_source=newsletter&utm_medium=email&utm_campaign=more_than_a_trillion_dollars_of_corporate_profit_smuggled_into_tax_havens&utm_term=2020-07-31

Tokar, D. 2020a. "U.K.'s Serious Fraud Office Charges Former Executives of G4S Subsidiary." *Wall Street Journal*, September 8, 2020. https://wsj.com/articles/u-k-s-serious-fraud-office-charges-former-executives-of-g4s-subsidiary-11599597317?st=kfus8bgky7luabq

Tokar, D. 2020b. "Accountant Pleads Guilty Ahead of Trial in Panama Papers Case." *Wall Street Journal*, February 28, 2020. https://wsj.com/articles/accountant-pleads-guilty-ahead-of-trial-in-panama-papers-case-11582931461?shareToken=ste59c1c4f300e4490ac6570a0ee554306

Transactional Records Access Clearinghouse at Syracuse University (TRACfed). 2020. "Criminal Enforcement." https://tracfed.syr.edu/

Tudor, K. 2019. "Symbolic Survival and Harm: Serious Fraud and Consumer Capitalism's Perversion of the Causa Sui Project." *The British Journal of Criminology* 59, no. 5, pp. 1237–53. https://doi.org/10.1093/bjc/azz009

U.K. Department for International Development. 2015. "Why Corruption Matters: Understanding Causes, Effects and How to Address them." *Department for International Development*, January 2015. https://assets.publishing.service.gov.uk/government/uploads/system/uploads/attachment_data/file/406346/corruption-evidence-paper-why-corruption-matters.pdf

United Nations Office on Drugs and Crime. 2010. "The Globalization of Crime." https://unodc.org/documents/data-and-analysis/tocta/TOCTA_Report_2010_low_res.pdf?bcsi_scan_E6B5D3DA0AAC65B7=0&bcsi_scan_filename=TOCTA_Report_2010_low_res.pdf

United Nations Office on Drugs and Crime. 2011. "Estimating Illicit Financial Flows Resulting from Drug Trafficking and other Transnational Organized Crimes." https://unodc.org/documents/data-and-analysis/Studies/Illicit_financial_flows_2011_web.pdf

United Nations Office on Drugs and Crime. 2013. "Combating Transnational Organized Crime Committed at Sea." https://unodc.org/documents/organized-crime/GPTOC/Issue_Paper_-_TOC_at_Sea.pdf

United Nations Office on Drugs and Crime. 2018. "Convention against Transnational Organized Crime and the Protocols Thereto." https://unodc.org/unodc/en/organized-crime/intro/UNTOC.html

United Nations Office on Drugs and Crime. 2019. "Money-laundering." https://unodc.org/e4j/en/organized-crime/module-4/key-issues/money-laundering.html

U.S. Attorney's Office Central District of California. "Federal Indictment Alleges Scheme to Avoid Payment of $1.8 Billion in Anti-Dumping Duties on Chinese Aluminum Imported as 'Pallets'." https://justice.gov/usao-cdca/pr/federal-indictment-alleges-scheme-avoid-payment-18-billion-anti-dumping-duties-chinese

U.S. Department of Justice Office of the Inspector General. 2004. "The Internal Effects of the Federal Bureau of Investigation's Reprioritization." *Audit Report 04–39*, September 2004. https://oig.justice.gov/reports/FBI/a0439/final.pdf

U.S. Department of the Treasury. 2011. "Fact sheet: Overview of Section 311 of the USA Patriot Act." https://treasury.gov/press-center/press-releases/Pages/tg1056.aspx

U.S. Immigration and Customs Enforcement. 2019. "IPR Center Reports Counterfeit Seizures Rise to $1.4 Billion." https://ice.gov/news/releases/ipr-center-reports-counterfeit-seizures-rise-14-billion

Vande Walle, G. 2002. "'The Collar Makes the Difference' - Masculine Criminology and Its Refusal to Recognise Markets as Criminogenic." *Crime, Law and Social Change* 37, no. 3, pp. 277–91.

Van Duyne, P.C., and T. Vander Beken. 2009. "The Incantations of the EU Organised Crime Policy Making." *Crime, Law and Social Change* 51, no. 2, pp. 261–81.

Varese, F. 2012. "How Mafias Take Advantage of Globalization." *The British Journal of Criminology* 52, no. 2, pp. 235–53.

Varraich, A. 2014. "Corruption: An Umbrella Concept." *University of Gothenburg*, June 2014. https://qog.pol.gu.se/digitalAssets/1551/1551604_2014_05_varraich.pdf

Von Lampe, K. 2001. "Not a Process of Enlightenment: The Conceptual History of Organized Crime in Germany and the United States of America." *Forum on Crime and Society* 1, no. 2, pp. 99–116. https://unodc.org/pdf/crime/publications/forum1vol2.pdf

Von Lampe, K. n.d. "U.S. Congress and Organized Crime." http://organized-crime.de/congoc.htm

Von Lampe, K. 2012. "Transnational Organized Crime Challenges for Future Research." *Crime, Law and Social Change* 58, no. 2, pp. 179–94.

Von Lampe, K. 2016. *Organized Crime.* Thousand Oaks: SAGE Publications.

Wainwright, T. 2016. *Narco-nomics How to Run a Drug Cartel.* New York, NY: PublicAffairs.

Weiser, B. 1997. "Brokers and Mob Linked in Swindle." *New York Times*, November 26, 1997. https://nytimes.com/1997/11/26/nyregion/brokers-and-mob-linked-in-swindle.html

Wells, D. 2009. "Burning Question: Was Hendrix Murdered?" *The Times (London, England)*, July 4, 2009. https://thetimes.co.uk/article/was-jimi-hendrix-murdered-x9sclmwvq35

Weinstein, H. 1989. "U.S. Indicts 3 on Music 'Payola,' Fraud Charges." *Los Angeles Times*, December 1, 1989. https://latimes.com/archives/la-xpm-1989-12-01-mn-140-story.html

Whaley, B, J. Busby. 2000. "Detecting deception: Practice, Practitioners, and Theory." *Trends in Organized Crime* 6, no. 1, pp. 73–105. https://doi-org.ez.lib.jjay.cuny.edu/10.1007/s12117-000-1007-x

White, R. 2016. "Building NESTs to Combat Environmental Crime Networks." *Trends in Organized Crime* 19, no. 1, pp. 88–105. doi:10.1007/s12117-015-9261-0

Williams, P. 2001. "Transnational Criminal Networks." In *Networks and Netwars: The Future of Terror, Crime, and Militancy*, ed. J. Arquilla and D. Ronfeldt, pp. 61–97. Santa Monica, CA: RAND Corporation. https://rand.org/pubs/monograph_reports/MR1382.html Also available in print form.

Williams, T.C. 2020. "Triangulation." *Harper's Magazine*, August 2020.

Windle, J., and A. Silke. 2019. "Is Drawing from the State 'State of the Art'?: A Review of Organised Crime Research Data Collection and Analysis, 2004–2018." *Trends in Organized Crime* 22, no. 4, pp. 394–413. doi:10.1007/s12117-018-9356-5

Wolverton, R.A. 2012. "What CPAs Need to Know About Organized Crime." *Journal of Accountancy*, April 1, 2012. https://journalofaccountancy.com/issues/2012/apr/20114853.html

Woodiwiss, M. 2015a. "Questioning Preconceived Notions about Organized Crime: An Interview with Petrus C. van Duyne." *Trends in Organized Crime* 18, nos. 1–2, pp. 118–27. doi:10.1007/s12117-015-9244-1

Woodiwiss, M. 2015b. "The Analysis and Containment of Organized Crime in New York City and Beyond: An Interview with James B. Jacobs." *Trends in Organized Crime* 18, no. 1–2, pp. 86–93.

Woodiwiss, M. 2017. *Double Crossed the Failure of Organized Crime Control*. London: Pluto Press.

World Customs Organization. 2019. "Money Laundering and Terrorist Financing." http://wcoomd.org/en/topics/enforcement-and-compliance/activities-and-programmes/money-laundering-and-terrorist-financing.aspx

World Heritage Encyclopedia. 2020. "Valachi Hearings." http://self.gutenberg.org/articles/Valachi_hearings

Young, M.A., and M. Woodiwiss. 2020. "A World Fit for Money Laundering: The Atlantic Alliance's Undermining of Organized Crime Control." *Trends in Organized Crime* (online), April 25, 2020. https://doi.org/10.1007/s12117-020-09386-8

Zelikow, P., E. Edelman, K. Harrison, and C.W. Gventer. 2020. "The Risk of Strategic Corruption: How States Weaponize Graft." *Foreign Affairs*, July/August 2020. https://foreignaffairs.com/articles/united-states/2020-06-09/rise-strategic-corruption

About the Author

David M. Shapiro serves as a Distinguished Lecturer, Deputy Director of the Saturday MPA program, and Coordinator of the Fraud Examination and Financial Forensics (undergraduate) programs at the City University of New York's John Jay College of Criminal Justice. Formerly, he was Deputy Director of the Advanced Certificate in Forensic Accounting (MPA) program at John Jay College of Criminal Justice. He provides instruction in fraud examination, financial forensics, and managerial inspection and oversight related courses at the graduate and undergraduate levels presently under the Department of Public Management and formerly under the Department of Economics.

Among the courses taught by David are accounting information systems; advanced auditing; public sector inspection and oversight; fiscal management and capital and operational budgeting; public sector accounting and auditing; forensic accounting; public administration; advanced financial reporting; managerial accounting; financial accounting; intermediate accounting; forensic financial analysis; corporate and white-collar crime; bureau pathology; and compliance and ethics for auditors.

He has published articles in the areas of accounting, finance, and risk management. Among his published works is a special chapter for the book *How They Got Away with It: White Collar Criminals and the Financial Meltdown.*

David is a financial and nonfinancial enhanced due diligence specialist. He is also an expert on financial investigations and law enforcement. His extensive background includes work as an FBI special agent and assistant legal advisor, an assistant prosecutor in Essex County, NJ, and the global practice leader at Aon's corporate investigative solutions—where he led investigations of financial crimes. He has worked as a management consultant, bankruptcy restructuring associate, independent private sector monitor/inspector general, certified public accountant, insurance claims investigator, and internal controls specialist. Additionally, he served under federal monitorships of various organized crime groups in the New York City metropolitan area, auditing, investigating, and evaluating compliance with federal, state, and local laws and contractual agreements with private businesses and public agencies.

In brief, David has focused on conduct and financial crime risks, including the use of financial metrics to prevent, detect, and respond to organizational and occupational frauds and organized economic crimes impacting domestic and foreign commerce.

Index

www.ingramcontent.com/pod-product-compliance
Lightning Source LLC
Chambersburg PA
CBHW061306220326
41599CB00026B/4761